Siya Kolisi

Against All Odds

Siya Kolisi

Against All Odds

Jeremy Daniel

Jonathan Ball Publishers

Johannesburg & Cape Town

Published in South Africa in 2019 by
JONATHAN BALL PUBLISHERS
A division of Media24 (Pty) Ltd
PO Box 33977
Jeppestown
2043

ISBN 978-1-86842-982-0
ebook ISBN 978-1-86842-983-7

*Every effort has been made to trace the copyright holders and
to obtain their permission for the use of copyright material. The
publishers apologise for any errors or omissions and would be grateful
to be notified of any corrections that should be incorporated in future
editions of this book.*

Twitter: www.twitter.com/JonathanBallPub
Facebook: www.facebook.com/JonathanBallPublishers
Blog: http://jonathanball.bookslive.co.za/

Cover image: Siya Kolisi leads a media conference at
the Pullman Paris Centre Hotel, Paris, 9 November 2018
(Photo by Steve Haag/Gallo Images)

Cover by MR Design
Design and typesetting by Triple M Design
Set in 10/16pt Ionic MT Regular

Contents

Part 3

Prologue

Green and gold. Twenty-three crisp uniforms hang in a locked change room, ready for the squad. Each jersey is identical, but one of them is historic. After 480 internationals, today, 9 June 2018, one will be worn by the first black Springbok captain.

That Saturday morning, the day began when the minivan carrying the Springbok logistics team pulled into the parking lot as the first pale rays of a wintry sun lit up Ellis Park Stadium.

In the front seat was JJ Fredericks, the 48-year-old former flanker and Springbok logistics manager. He was responsible for making sure everything was perfect for the team when they arrived before a game.

On match days, JJ has a ritual. He gets up at 5 am for a quick gym session, then has breakfast at the hotel, before heading off to work.

By 8.30 that morning, the logistics team was carrying the overstuffed kit bag through the echoing bowels of the massive concrete stadium towards the change rooms, and running through the pre-game routine. While JJ and his assistant laid out the match kit for every single player in the squad, Vivian Verwant, the physiotherapist, prepared a medical station and Lindsay Weyer set up the video feed and the communications system that the management team would use to stay in touch as they criss-crossed the stadium later in the day.

Rugby has always been part of JJ's life. 'I was the first black captain of a provincial franchise at the Griffons,' he explains from his office at SA Rugby, where he is busy preparing for the 2019 Rugby World Cup in Japan.

He joined SA Rugby as a driver for the Springbok squad gathered in Cape Town ahead of the 2007 World Cup, then slowly worked his way up to become tour manager of the Under-20 team before becoming the Springbok logistics manager.

On that cold winter morning, the Springboks were preparing to play England at Ellis Park. It was a crucial fixture for both sides. The logistics team worked quickly, setting out the uniforms in numerical order from 1 to 23: two shirts for each player, one hanging up and one folded on a bench, a pair of shorts and socks, towel and commemorative pennant with the details of the game on it. Players are always responsible for their own personal items, including boots.

The level of preparation for an international rugby match in 2018 would have been unimaginable to the earliest Springboks. For the first five games the national team ever played, against a touring English side in 1891 and then in 1896, the South Africans wore whatever they could lay their hands on. They lost both games of the first tour and the first three games of the second tour. Ahead of the fourth Test of the second tour, at Newlands, one of their star players, Barry Heatlie, headed off to the Old Diocesan club, known today simply as Bishops, and gathered up 15 myrtle-green club jerseys for the South African team to wear.

That historic sixth encounter between South Africa and England was the first victory ever recorded by a South African team, and the first time that 'the colony' had triumphed over 'the motherland'. Although the nickname 'Springboks' would only be adopted ten years later, the green jerseys have been worn ever since that first win.

By 9.30 am, the dressing room was ready for the players and the coach. Before locking up, JJ paused and ran his hand over the number 6 jersey. As a flanker himself, and as the first black man ever to captain a Currie Cup side, it had special significance. Not to mention that this was the place where Nelson Mandela had worn Francois Pienaar's number 6 during the historic 1995 Rugby World Cup final.

Every Springbok jersey is embroidered with the statistics of the player who will wear it. On that day, the captain's jersey simply read:

Siyamthanda Kolisi
South Africa vs England
9 June 2018
Johannesburg
29th Cap

Part 1

1
■

Trial by Fire

Siya Kolisi kept his emotions under wraps as he walked out into the roar of the stadium. It was the 26-year-old's first game as Springbok captain. He let out a slow, controlled breath and clasped the hand of the young fan accompanying him onto the field. There was no denying the electricity in the air and the significance of the moment.

Out on the field, his Springbok team-mates approached him one by one for a hug or a quick fist bump to let him know they understood what a big day it was.

Being the first black Springbok captain was not the only milestone that day. Siya tried to acknowledge the moment for all the players, and to let them know this was not only about him. This day felt like a fresh start for rugby in South Africa. Promising young stars such as Sibusiso 'Sbu' Nkosi, RG Snyman and Aphiwe Dyantyi were making their Test debuts, while Tendai 'Beast' Mtawarira was just one game away from being the first black African to play 100 Tests for South Africa. The first game of the 2018 England tour was also of vital importance for the new coach, Rassie Erasmus, and for a nation desperate to regain its stature as a rugby powerhouse.

Siya draped an arm around his vice-captain, Eben Etzebeth, while the players lined up for the singing of the national anthem. He shut his eyes tightly, threw back his head, and let the lyric and melody consume him and build slowly up to the stirring ending ...

Let us live and strive for freedom in South Africa, our land.

On the stroke of 5 pm, referee Matthew Carley blew the whistle, millions around the world tuned in on television, the crowd in the stadium roared with anticipation, and it was game on.

Boxing legend Mike Tyson famously said that 'everyone has a plan until they get punched in the face'. The Springboks wanted to overwhelm the opposition with speed and power, apply sustained pressure, and rack up a famous victory for their new captain and coach. That plan started to unravel in the first two minutes.

England were ranked fourth in the world at the time, and had been improving steadily under the guidance of coach Eddie Jones. The team were unbeaten through 2016, they had won the Six Nations Championship, and they had recently equalled the world record of 18 games undefeated. But three successive defeats coming into this game had shaken their self-belief, and they were determined to get their campaign back on a winning track.

In the first minute of the game, the Springbok scrumhalf Faf de Klerk fed the ball out to RG Snyman, who gathered it cleanly and then went to ground. De Klerk jumped right back in, cleaning up and passing to flyhalf Handre Pollard, who was tackled hard. Jean-Luc du Preez charged into the ruck, but he was judged to be off his feet and conceded a penalty.

It was 61 metres to the goalposts, but at this altitude England fullback Elliot Daly was unfazed by the distance. The ball soared high in the thin Highveld air, then dropped just over the posts to give England three precious points in the first two minutes of the game.

Following the restart, the Boks were quickly forced on the defensive. England whipped the ball down their advancing backline with a series of quick passes until it was in the hands of winger Mike Brown, who bent low to gather the ball, beat two tackles, and scrambled over into the corner for an England try.

Daly sent the ball back over the posts with his second kick of the match, and in the first five minutes of the game, Siya and his team found themselves already down by ten points and staring defeat in the face.

Although reeling from these opening blows, the Springboks managed to settle and take the game to their opponents with an attack that led to a penalty, off which Handre Pollard collected three points. But the English onslaught was far from over and the Springbok defence was leaking badly. Once again, England built up pressure through ten phases of play that took them over the Springbok 22-metre line. The defence had lost its shape and cohesion and England knew it. Another series of neat passes down the backline released Elliot Daly, who sliced through the defence like a game knife carving through fresh Springbok biltong.

'Another beautifully constructed England try,' announced the local television commentator grudgingly.

Silence settled over the stadium, followed by some muted applause from the stunned home crowd. The fans had been sold the idea of a fresh start for Springbok rugby, but it appeared they would be getting a bruising defeat with a side order of humiliation instead.

The try was converted easily and the scoreboard broadcast the shame to anyone brave enough to look up: 17–3 to the visitors with over an hour left to play.

This was not the start that Siya or Rassie wanted. This untested Springbok team was now facing overwhelming odds, and England were fired up. The hits just kept on coming.

England won some more possession following a breakdown on the halfway line. The flyhalf, George Ford, looked up and to his right where he spotted Jonny May charging down the wing. He floated a perfect high pass that left three Springbok defenders flat-footed. May collected in one easy motion and charged forward before flipping an inside pass to the captain, Owen Farrell, who seemed genuinely surprised at how much space he had and cantered over easily for England's third try.

Twenty-one points down in the first quarter of the match. One-way traffic. The Springboks were embarrassed, avoiding eye contact and unsure of how to respond.

Siya gathered his players together behind the posts for a team talk. As they waited for England to convert two more points, he spoke to the team, trying to calm them down and get them to remember why they were out there and what they were trying to do. He wasn't the type of captain known for his passionate speeches, preferring to lead by example, but he understood this was a moment that required firm leadership. Time was still on their side if they began the turnaround right then.

The overworked scoreboard ticked up again, registering 24 points to 3.

What the team needed was for someone to step up and

announce themselves. To create a special moment that would revive the team's confidence. Slowly, they began to develop an attacking position down the right wing … winger Sbu Nkosi charged hard at the England defence, going down just metres from the corner flag. The ball popped out of the ruck and Faf de Klerk waited a few seconds before picking it up. Looking around, he saw the England lock Maro Itoje lose his footing and tumble to the ground, creating a small gap. De Klerk burst through and hurled himself towards the try line just a few metres away. With two pairs of strong arms trying to hold him back, he managed to wriggle free and strain forwards to score the Springboks' first try. Now it was 24–8, and a sense of relief rolled across the stadium like thunder from a Highveld storm.

Sbu Nkosi could feel the relief. He was making his debut for the Boks that day. Having grown up in the small town of Barberton, Nkosi had left home at the end of Grade 9 to attend one of South Africa's legendary rugby schools, Jeppe High School for Boys in Johannesburg. He was having an excellent season for the Sharks, which had led to his inclusion in the South African squad.

In the 29th minute of the game, Nkosi was prowling on the wing, waiting for an opportunity, when he saw Faf de Klerk break with the ball, then find Damian de Allende, who beat his man. Sbu accelerated towards the line and gathered the perfect pass, but he was being hustled hard towards the touch-line, so he dropped the ball onto his right foot, punted it gently forward over the try line, and chased hard. Daly, the England fullback, came charging in at speed but overshot the ball and it bobbled enticingly in the end zone for Nkosi, who just managed to drop a hand on it and score his first try for the Boks.

'I thought he'd made the wrong decision,' said the commentator. 'He kicked it a little bit far, the bounce was a bit fortunate ... followed up well ... there's no doubt he's grounded it and that is a super try for Sbu Nkosi.'

Just like that, it was a different game. The momentum had swung 180 degrees. The Springboks had found their belief again and wild horses could not keep them out. In the 33rd minute, Sbu Nkosi combined with another debutant, Aphiwe Dyantyi, to go over the line for a beautiful third try. Dyantyi's meteoric rise was one of the stories of the season. He had been long considered too small, and had basically given up on rugby until he went to the University of Johannesburg, where his star began to rise and rise.

From feeling like they were down and out, suddenly the Boks were back to within four points of the lead. It was England's turn to look shell-shocked.

The relief in the stadium turned to excitement and then transformed again into real belief that the Boks could come back and win this thing.

Faf de Klerk was having the game of his life. Two minutes before half-time he picked up from the base of the scrum, accelerated, and combined with Pollard, who offloaded a long pass to fullback Willie le Roux. Nkosi was right there in support in case he was needed, but Le Roux had transformed into a freight train, crashing over the line to score. From being down 24–3 and out of it, the Springboks went into half-time 29–27 ahead.

It's not hard to imagine that the half-time talk Rassie Erasmus delivered was very different to what it would have been 15 minutes earlier.

After the heart-stopping drama of the first half, the second half resembled a normal game of rugby. Advantage swung back and forth between the two teams and it was unclear which side was going to stamp its authority on the game. Pollard added another three points via a penalty before England's big prop Mako Vunipola was sent off for a late hit on Faf de Klerk, and the Springboks seized the advantage.

Ten metres from the try line, Siya picked up the ball from the ruck and drove hard, making valuable ground and pulling defenders with him, inching closer and closer to the try line. It was a powerful charge from the captain, and the crowd willed him forward. Again, Faf de Klerk managed to keep it alive, finding RG Snyman, who in turn passed to Aphiwe Dyantyi, who fumbled the ball before grasping it gratefully and diving over into the corner. There was pandemonium in the stadium, but at 39 points to 32 the result was still up in the air before another penalty extended the Springbok advantage.

With ten minutes left to play, England scored one last try and the game was poised yet again, at 42–39, but as the clock ran down, the Springboks hung on for dear life.

It had taken everything out of them, and it could easily have gone the other way, but they had bounced back to record a famous victory for the new captain, the new coach and the long-suffering Springbok fans.

In a lifetime spent on the rugby field, this was surely the greatest high that Siya Kolisi had ever experienced. After a win like this, anything felt possible.

2

■

The Early Days

In May 1995, when Siya was almost four years old, the third Rugby World Cup, hosted by South Africa, kicked off with unprecedented excitement and fanfare. The Springboks had been barred from playing in the first two editions of the tournament due to the apartheid-era sports boycott, but this was a new era of reconciliation and nation-building and the country was eager to host a major global sporting event. The first democratic elections, held in April 1994, had been a great success and South Africa felt like a country reborn.

Everything and anything felt possible in 1995, even in a place like Zwide, a flat and dusty township on the outskirts of Port Elizabeth, where the apartheid government's utter disdain for the residents, along with a chronic lack of investment, social services and opportunity, had stranded the people in a seemingly endless cycle of poverty and unemployment.

Sport was a relief and a distraction from these bleak conditions. While soccer was the only game that mattered in most parts of the country, rugby was the prestige game in this part of the Eastern Cape, and the communities of Port Elizabeth were proud of their non-racial rugby history and the quality of their teams, such as the African Bombers and Spring Rose.

Siyamthanda Kolisi was born at Zwide's Dora Nginza Hospital on 16 June 1991, the son of Fezakele Kolisi and Phakama Qasana. Phakama was only a schoolgirl of 16 when she had her baby, and was unable to meet the demands of caring for a child. So, the decision was made that Siyamthanda would go to live with Nolulamile Kolisi, his grandmother on his father's side, in Mthembu Street.

Money was desperately tight. Hunger and poverty stalked the streets of Zwide. The two-roomed house where Siya and his grandmother lived was cold during the winter and boiling hot in summer. The roof leaked when it rained, and when the wind blew through the streets, curtains of sand settled everywhere.

'Sometimes I wouldn't eat, but my gran would go to a friend and bring back a slice of bread for me,' Kolisi told journalist Angus Powers in a feature story, 'African Bomber: The True Story of Siya Kolisi'. 'Sometimes she wouldn't eat for a while, because whatever she got she gave to us.'

Every day, his grandmother made the long journey to the lush suburbs where she had a job as a domestic worker. Life was hard, and people longed for a distraction and some good news. The 1995 World Cup was perfectly poised to deliver exactly that.

Siya was too young to understand the rules of the game, or the impact that the young All Blacks winger Jonah Lomu was about to make. But when New Zealand lined up against Ireland in one of the first games in Group C, he wasn't too young to understand the power of the haka, the pre-match challenge that every All Blacks team lays down to its opponents just before the whistle.

Siya was transfixed, and immediately began to learn how to

do the haka, together with a group of neighbourhood friends. 'Each time I returned from work, he would wait for me at the gate and demonstrate how the haka was performed,' his father told the *Weekend Post* many years later.

When the Springboks won that tournament, it was a turning point for the game in South Africa. The fact that Nelson Mandela donned the Springbok jersey and threw his reputation behind the team opened the floodgates, and the celebrations that swept the nation after the victory in the World Cup final were felt in every community. For the first time, the national team was embraced by the black majority, and the popularity of rugby soared.

Around the time of the World Cup, Siya's father moved to Cape Town to look for more regular work. It was a tough blow for a child already living with the absence of his mother. One of the things that the father passed on to his son was an early love of the game. Fezakele had played centre when he was younger, and many of the men in the family were rugby players. He liked to speak to Siya about his playing days, and also about his father, Jan, who had been a respected flanker in his time but had died at the age of 36.

Siya's grandmother enrolled him at the local school, Ntyatyambo Primary. Although it was poor and lacking resources, the school took good care of its pupils, and young Siya fitted in easily with the other children from the neighbourhood, learning to read and write and being promoted with his grade. It's safe to say that school was a sanctuary from the instability and poverty that confronted Siya at every turn.

On the nights when their electricity was cut off due to non-payment, Siya would take his homework out into the street and crouch under the streetlights to see what he was doing.

When there was no food for dinner, he would drink extra glasses of water just to fill his stomach. There was a constant, low-level anxiety around where the next meal was coming from, and in his immediate environment many children responded to hunger with depression, anger or violence.

Siya didn't have his own bedroom, so every night he would take a pair of cushions off the sofa to make up a little bed next to the front door, where he slept. He had to sleep lightly in case an aunt or uncle came barging in late at night and the door smacked him on the head. In the mornings, he would pick up the cushions and remake the sofa before heading off to school.

There were seldom grown-ups around to look after Siya. His grandmother left early for the city, his mother appeared only occasionally, and his father was away in Cape Town for long stretches of time. Siya was left unsupervised as a child, and he was simply forced to make his own way in the world. 'I was very poor. I had no toys,' he remembered. 'I used to use a brick and pretend it was a car. But, *sjoe*, I would drive that brick. It was the best thing ever.'

Like most young children living in poverty in South African townships, there is very little documented about Siya's early life. How did Siya first become aware of the African Bombers? Probably through his father. How did he join the club and begin to play with them? It's hard to know. Perhaps one sunny afternoon when Siya was ten years old, he decided not to go straight home after school. After all, there was nobody waiting for him, and there was nothing to do. Perhaps he set off down Koyana Street, past the roundabout and along the long, grey concrete wall covered with fading advertisements for artists and mechanics, plumbers, painters and other services.

If a game was on, then he would have heard a loud cheer

from behind the concrete wall and looked up just in time to see a rugby ball flying through the air and hitting one of the faded white rugby goalposts that peeked over the wall. As the cheers turned to groans, Siya would have been drawn towards the action, wanting to find out more.

Carrying on walking until he found a small hole in the fence around the Ndzondelelo High School sports fields, Siya would have been small enough to squeeze through the gap, past the schoolboys sharing a smoke at the bottom of the field, and to keep on going until finally he came round the corner and spotted the gate into the Dan Qeqe Stadium.

Climbing up the dirt embankment around the pitch, Siya would have looked down onto the green rugby field to see the African Bombers senior team playing a full-contact practice match. Edging closer, he would have seen the players whipping the ball down the backline and running towards the opposition.

If a voice had begun shouting instructions, he would have turned to see the Bombers coach, Eric Songwiqi, down on the touchline watching the game so intently that he didn't even notice the young child nearby.

If the ball went rolling down the embankment, Siya would have jumped to his feet to fetch it and run it over to the coach.

Perhaps Eric thanked him and asked a few questions about who he was and where he went to school. One thing we know for sure: when Eric saw the passion for the game in Siya's eyes, he suggested that he should come and join the junior Bombers for their next practice.

The African Bombers are a legendary rugby club in the area. Founded in 1954, the club managed to keep playing rugby all through the apartheid years and turning out players of incredible quality, despite the fact that there was no chance of their having a career in rugby. They did it for the love of the game.

All age groups were represented at African Bombers. Players could join the club at Under-11 level and then move up through the ranks from Under-13 to Under-15 and all the way up to the senior levels. It was an impressive rugby organisation with a proud history, and it was all run on a shoestring budget.

Eric didn't need to ask twice. From the very next practice, Siya was the first to arrive and the last to leave. He worked hard and he was open to taking direction from the coach. Among the boys in the team, there was one in particular who impressed Siya. His name was Zolani Faku, the team's hooker, and Siya was fairly certain that he'd never seen a stronger kid than Zolani. Siya was still quite small and slight, and when he had the misfortune to be tackled by Zolani in practice, it was something he remembered for a very long time. But when he scrummed alongside him, it felt like his team was unstoppable.

Eric noticed the connection between Siya and Zolani early on, and he often paired them up, watching with pleasure as they brought out the best in one another. He also gave Siya an old pair of rugby boots to train in. Those boots meant the world to Siya and he wore them as often as he could.

After a few weeks of training, Eric decided to find out more about Siya, so he accompanied him on his walk home and tried to learn more about his life outside of rugby. Siya was a bit vague with his answers, but Eric could tell that there was not a lot of structure in his life. Slowly, he was able to get Siya to open up.

Eric's day job was as principal at Emsengeni Primary School, and he had a strong feeling that Siya would flourish in that environment. 'I could see the destiny in sport of Siya,' Eric told an interviewer in 2018, 'from the time he was a young boy.' He suggested to Siya that perhaps he should ask his guardians if he could transfer from Ntyatyambo Primary to Emsengeni Primary. That way, he reasoned, he would be able to keep a closer eye on the youngster and help him develop as a player and as a person.

It's easy to imagine the suggestion as just a throwaway comment from an adult to a child, but it had profound implications for Siya. He seized on the offer like a lifeline in the middle of a stormy ocean. An adult that he really respected had made a suggestion and shown him a path, and he wasn't about to let it go. He ran home as fast as he could to tell his grandmother the news.

Eric had assumed that Siya would enrol at the beginning of the new school year. He didn't expect the boy to show up at Emsengeni Primary the very next day.

But if enthusiasm was one of the traits that Eric was looking for, then Siya had it by the bucketload, and this kind of commitment was something that Eric liked to honour in the children that he worked with. It took a few days to complete the paperwork, and for Siya's father to come over and register him for the new school, but by the end of the week, Siya had transferred to Emsengeni Primary School and, in so doing, changed the course of his life.

3

■

The Journey Begins

Siya slipped on his shiny black school shoes and tugged his grey trousers down as far as they could go. The trousers were too short and he didn't want everyone to know that he wasn't wearing socks because he didn't own any. The shoes had been passed down from a neighbour who had outgrown them long ago, and his grandmother had spent so long polishing them that they looked practically new.

Siya had learned quickly that the teachers at Emsengeni Primary were strict about uniform: white-collared shirt, dark green jersey and long grey trousers for the boys, and mustard-yellow dress over a crisp white shirt and long green socks for the girls – with no exceptions.

Siya was 12 years old when he entered Emsengeni Primary in 2003. Coming into Grade 6 as a new boy wasn't easy. Siya had to catch up quickly with the higher standard of schoolwork, adapt to the new environment at the school, and try to make new friends. There were nearly 700 children at Emsengeni and many of them had been there since Grade 1, so their friendships were already well established. But they were very accepting of him, and Siya gradually settled in.

He was keen to show what he could do on the rugby field, but the school 'field' was barren and hard, made up of red dirt that was scattered with pebbles and surrounded by a high wire fence. Anything more than touch rugby on this surface was only for the foolish or the very brave. There was a real incentive to learn how to avoid tackles, because if you had the misfortune to fall on the unforgiving surface, then there was a good chance that your uniform would be ruined and you would go home covered in blood.

Luckily, the field wasn't the only place to play at Emsengeni. There was a small patch of thick grass that ran between the classroom blocks, with two large trees at either end. This was where the rugby-crazy boys gathered to play, dashing around, kicking and chasing a soft ball, and getting into rolling mauls that would carry on and on until the bell rang to signal the end of break.

Those early games of break-time rugby gave Siya a way to make some friends. One of the Grade 6 boys, Phaphama Hoyi, also played with Siya at African Bombers. Everyone who watched him play thought he was a rising star. He was lightning fast, had great hands, and possessed a wicked sidestep that he used to get out of trouble easily. He often left Siya grasping at thin air as he dodged past him to score.

Emsengeni was the most fun and nurturing environment that Siya had ever experienced, and he thrived during that year at the primary school. 'He loved to laugh,' recalls Lulama Magxaki, one of his teachers, 'but I could never hear what he was saying. He just spoke quietly and made those around him laugh.'

One of the most important changes in Siya's life was the introduction of the national school feeding scheme. In 2002, the government introduced a programme to provide a basic meal to every student at a no-fee school across South Africa, without exception. It's hard to exaggerate the significance of this development for Siya, and for so many children like him, who had only known life on the poverty line. Feeling secure in the knowledge that he would eat a meal at school at least once a day was a profound change for him.

If there was nothing to eat for breakfast at home, then he would count down the minutes to first break at 10.30, when a plate of chicken with samp or rice would be served to each of the learners at the school. Of course, on its own this wasn't nearly enough for a growing boy, but it was better than nothing, and there certainly were days when that meal at school was the only proper meal he would eat. All over Zwide, on a daily basis, people were struggling to get by. Yet, despite the poverty, people would readily share what little they had. Zwide could be a very tough environment, but there were also tremendous acts of selflessness and generosity between neighbours every single day.

Nolulamile Kolisi had lived a hard life. She had had to fight for everything in a world where the odds were stacked against her. Siya would have been too young to understand that her health was fragile and that she was carrying a burden too heavy for her to bear much longer.

His life finally had some direction, and Siya had found a father figure in Eric Songwiqi. Aside from his advice on the rugby field, Eric kept an eye on Siya and made sure that he was all right. 'This was a disciplined boy, dedicated to what he was doing,' said Eric. He could see an open-heartedness and a willingness to trust in Siya that was so genuine and heartfelt that it was impossible to ignore. Siya was hungry to improve himself, and it showed in everything that he did.

Not everyone remembers Siya as having a passion for rugby. One of his teachers laughs when she tells how she sometimes used to find him hiding in the boys' bathroom on cold days before rugby practice. She used to tear a switch from a nearby tree and threaten to beat any boys who weren't out on the field in a few minutes' time. With that kind of persuasion, attendance at games and at practice was high ... and with a coach like Eric Songwiqi to motivate them, the boys of Zwide township improved fast.

Many of them were playing for both the school team and the African Bombers junior teams. Sometimes there were games for the school team in the morning, and then club games in the afternoon.

It was a lot to handle but Siya didn't mind at all. In fact, he thrived on it. The instability of his home life had given him a longing for order and for clarity of purpose. He loved being part of a team, where he knew exactly what his role was, what the rules were, and that he could trust his team-mates.

While Eric played a pivotal role as a mentor and coach, the other members of the team were just as important. They were Siya's tribe, and he wasn't about to let them down. He wasn't the biggest player or the fastest player on the team, but he adapted quickly. Siya learned how to read the game, to contribute to the team effort, and ways to play strategically that set him apart from the players who were bigger and faster than him.

Siya's talent shone through right from the beginning. Eric spotted it and submitted the boy's name as one of the players for the Eastern Province Under-12 Interprovincial tournament.

Rugby was quickly becoming the most important part of

Siya's life. Passion for the game was widespread across Zwide. The small concrete grandstand at Dan Qeqe Stadium would fill up with spectators in the hours before a match. People would come to eat and drink, catch up with friends, and talk about the issues of the day. By the time the game began, they would be happy and excited and vocal in their support and opinions about the teams involved.

Siya loved the atmosphere in the stadium. The biggest game of the season was always against the Bombers' arch-rivals, Spring Rose, from New Brighton. When these two giants clashed, the stands would be packed and the fans would discuss the game for hours on end – before, during and after.

The big games at Dan Qeqe Stadium were occasions when Siya might see his father. If Fezakele was in town, he would probably attend a match, so Siya would keep an eye out for him. If he was there, they would sit together and comment on the action, and these were rare and precious times when Siya could really bond with his father.

4
∎

Everything Changes

Vincent Mai was born in 1940 in the farming district of Cradock. As a boy, he was sent off to Port Elizabeth to attend Grey High School and fell in love with the game of rugby. He did well enough at school to win a place at the University of Cape Town (UCT), where he continued to play rugby and earned a degree in accountancy.

In 1964, Vincent moved to London and embarked on a stellar career as a merchant banker on both sides of the Atlantic. But his heart remained in the Eastern Cape and with his high school, so as soon as he could, Vincent Mai established a bursary for underprivileged children to gain the opportunity to attend The Grey, as the school is affectionately known.

Vincent Mai's generosity and vision would have a profound effect on Siya's life.

In late 2003, that bursary plan began to take shape. Andrew Hayidakis was the senior sports master at Grey Junior. He was pleased when he found out that the school board and the principal were going ahead with the plan to bring in the first batch of 'development kids', as they were being called. A trio of boys from the underprivileged communities around Port

Elizabeth would be offered rugby scholarships to attend Grey Junior School for a year.

If the boys were successful at Grey, then there would be an option for them to continue into the adjoining high school, but for now they were just going to get the programme off the ground and see how it went. The school was looking at Andrew, as the Under-13 'A' rugby coach, to make some recommendations for players. He probably had more interactions with the communities of Zwide, Kwazakele and Kwamagxaki than did the staff from the arts and sciences faculties because rugby was so popular in this part of the country and Grey Junior played against many school rugby teams.

'Sir!' shouted a column of young boys in perfect unison, as they marched past in single file across the quadrangle. Andrew nodded and gave the traditional reply ... 'Boys!' They were all dressed in white shirts and shorts on their way to cricket practice. Andrew imagined it would be nice to have boys from different backgrounds in the social mix at Grey High School. It would be good for everyone, he decided.

Andrew knew exactly whom he would call in order to make this happen. Every time the Grey rugby teams played against teams coached by Eric Songwiqi, Andrew was impressed by the way they played the game and by the discipline that the boys displayed, both on and off the field. He picked up the phone and got hold of Eric in his office at Emsengeni Primary School.

They chatted for a while, and Andrew explained about the new programme and what Grey would be offering. Eric told him about some of the players he was coaching. After comparing their schedules, they realised that they would both be at the Eastern Province Interprovincial Under-12 trials in Mossel Bay in a few weeks' time. This was where Andrew would get a look at the boys that Eric had in mind.

When assistant coach Gary Carter arrived for a staff meeting, Andrew rang off and turned his attention back to the upcoming rugby tour to their old rivals, Grey College in Bloemfontein.

In Zwide, Eric hung up the phone and sat quietly in his dimly lit office, thinking about what he had just heard. Naturally, he was pleased that a few of his players would get to experience a life that was so rare in the townships of Port Elizabeth. On the other hand, he would be losing three of his best players to opposition teams, and that didn't sit well with a competitive coach who liked to win games. He knew his African Bombers team was good, and that it was well-balanced. It would be a big blow to the team to lose their star players, but he could never stand in anyone's way for something as life-changing as this.

On the way to rugby practice that afternoon, Eric decided that he wasn't going to tell any of the players about Grey Junior and their plans. It would put too much pressure on the players. There was too much at stake. It's one thing to be motivated about tactics and strategy on the field. That kind of pressure is helpful. But when a good performance could almost certainly lead to a good school, then university, a degree, a well-paid job, that was something else entirely. It was no exaggeration to say that each scholarship to Grey Junior and High School would change the destiny of whole families, who would be relying on their sons to help pull them out of poverty. This was not the kind of pressure you put on an 11-year-old boy ahead of a rugby match.

He decided he would just motivate them to play their hearts out as usual and leave it at that.

In the weeks leading up to the interprovincial trials, the African Bombers trained harder than ever. They were determined to show that their brand of rugby was as good as anyone else's.

* * *

Siya's grandmother had saved a pair of apples for him to take on the journey to Mossel Bay. This would be the furthest her grandson had ever travelled from home and it made her nervous. Despite her advanced years, she had hardly ever travelled outside the city and she struggled to find ways to advise him. She comforted herself with the fact that he was so excited about the trip, and that he would be back that same evening.

Siya had lain awake for hours listening to the wind and trying not to wake anyone up. The excitement of playing in the Eastern Province Under-12 trials was overwhelming. Part of him was dreading it; the other part couldn't wait for the sun to rise and the day to begin.

Next to Siya, a baby stirred, and he reached over instinctively to adjust its blanket and provide comfort.

A few weeks earlier, his mother had paid a visit to the house. She had brought a new baby with her, a six-month-old son that she had been raising but now wanted to leave in the care of Nolulamile in Mthembu Street. There had been a long argument between his mother and his grandmother, but when his mother finally left, the baby had stayed behind. His name was Liyema.

They had made a small space for Liyema to sleep and tried to make him as comfortable as possible. Slowly, the family got to know the baby and to include him in their lives.

It had taken Siya a while to learn what to do when the baby cried, and to learn all about his moods, but they had gotten used to one another and even started having some fun together. It was amazing to see Liyema grow so quickly. Siya began to look forward to seeing the infant when he got home, and a special bond developed between the two half-brothers.

Finally, a ray of sunlight appeared through the corrugated-iron panels of the roof. Siya got out of bed quietly and got ready for the trip. It would take them at least four hours to get to Mossel Bay, and they were leaving early to make sure they got there on time.

He filled a two-litre bottle with water, thanked his grandmother for the fruit and set off for the designated meeting point. One by one, the team members arrived, laughing and joking, and the group set off for Mossel Bay, about 350 kilometres away.

The team spirit on the bus that morning was excellent. The boys were laughing and singing along to music on the radio, arguing about their favourite teams and their favourite players, and looking forward to their first game. Even though they hardly knew each other and they came from different schools and different backgrounds, it already felt like some kind of a brotherhood, and Siya was a part of it.

This was the kind of nurturing and supportive environment in which he thrived, and he fell silent only when the Indian Ocean came into view as they sped along the N2. Of course, Siya had seen the sea before, but he had never really spent a day down at the beach with friends and family. Passing through Wilderness, he couldn't help noticing how much fun the young families on the beach were having. He longed to be able to do the same one day.

Sitting next to Siya was a boy called Nick Holton, and the two of them started chatting to pass the time on the long journey.

By the time the bus finally reached the sports fields in Mossel Bay, Siya's confidence had begun to desert him. This was not the kind of scene that the boys from Zwide were used to. Junior rugby matches in Zwide attracted some passionate fans, but never more than 50 at most. This was rugby on a different scale. Some of the schools had transported their whole student body along to the event, and they were lined up alongside the pitch in full uniform, chanting and cheering as their teams warmed up for the games.

Parents had set up gazebos and umbrellas with tables crammed with food and drinks; coaches with clipboards consulted their notes; and there was even a medical tent where bandages and Deep Heat were being applied to bruised young elbows and scraped knees. Meanwhile, Siya didn't even have a decent pair of shorts; he was playing in an old pair of boxer shorts.

The bus pulled up next to a line of gleaming white 4x4s. Eric noticed a defeated stare float across the eyes of some of his players. He imagined how it felt for them to see the vast resources the other teams were going to deploy against his boys. He knew there was a real danger it could overwhelm them.

But Eric had been in this position many times before and he had been expecting this reaction. It was natural, so he struck up a conversation with Siya, gently reminding him of all the games they had won and how it was the same game, played by the same rules, no matter whether you were playing at Twickenham or Dan Qeqe Stadium. They just had to do what they always did.

'It just hurts much less when you are tackled on these fields than it does on ours,' said someone from the back of the bus. That broke the tension and the boys packed up laughing. Then they made their way over to the fields. Siya caught up with Phaphama Hoyi and Zolani Faku and the three of them tried to figure out which province was wearing which uniform. Andrew Hayidakis was standing with some of the parents from Grey Junior who had also made the trip when he caught sight of Eric Songwiqi arriving with his Eastern Province team, and he jogged over to welcome him and meet the players.

The schedule for the day's games had been written in black marker pen on a school whiteboard and placed outside the change room tent. Boys from all the provincial teams were huddled around it, looking at the scores of the games that had been completed and discussing which teams were playing the best so far.

Border had won their first match, South Western Districts were busy with their first game but were leading easily, and the team from KwaZulu-Natal had lost their first game. Looking down the list, Siya saw their first game was less than 30 minutes away. His nerves tightened.

Eric caught up with his team and gave them a set of warm-up exercises to perform, then sent them on a jog around the fields. He was still wondering whether he should have told the boys that some of them would be eligible for scholarships to Grey, but it was too late to spring that on them now. They already had enough pressure to deal with.

As the referee blew his whistle for the game to start, Eric could see that his team were much more nervous and unsure of themselves than ever before. The unfamiliar surroundings and the obvious displays of wealth and privilege from most of the other teams at the trials were intimidating.

Eastern Province won the toss and elected to kick off. But their flyhalf tried to kick it too hard and the ball bounced along the ground and into the arms of the opposing lock, who barrelled forward, knocking over a few forwards before offloading neatly to the eighth man. Border were a well-drilled team and Eastern Province were simply overwhelmed as the Border forwards kept tight control of the ball and moved play up the field quickly. Siya threw himself into the tackles, then got up, chased back, and did it again, but it was no use. It wasn't long before Eastern Province had conceded their first try.

The Grey Junior parents and friends began shouting instructions and offering advice from the sidelines. Border rushed back to their half of the field and waited for the restart. Eric was frustrated and angry. He knew his team was better than this. They just needed some time to settle.

From the restart, the Border fullback took a good catch and then sent a mighty kick back over the heads of the Eastern Province players and followed it up with a hard tackle on Phaphama. He spilled the ball forward and the referee played advantage. The Border centre kicked the ball over the line and dived on top of it for more points. Again, the crowd went wild. From the corner of his eye, Eric could see that Andrew Hayidakis and Gary Carter were watching the game closely, and he knew they were trying to avoid eye contact with him.

After those early points, Eastern Province settled down and found their rhythm, but they were always on the back foot and the points total against them kept rising. By half-time they were 30 points down and had not yet come close to scoring.

33

Siya was furious as he walked off the field to get the half-time orange slices. Eastern Province may not have been the best team at the tournament, but they were definitely not this bad. But nothing the team tried was working; their passes were going to ground and they were missing simple tackles, and he wasn't sure why. The mood of the team was quiet and sullen as they stood around, catching their breath. While Eric made his way towards the team, Siya began to talk softly to them, encouraging them, and instructing them that they had to do better. He liked to be liked by everyone on the team, but this was a moment for some truth-talking. They needed to be motivated in a serious manner if they were going to salvage their reputations. Sure, it was only Under-12 rugby, but everyone at home would hear about it if they were humiliated.

By the time the team went back on the field, they were fired up and ready to compete. Siya made sure he was right under the kick that got the second half under way, and he gathered it tightly, then looked up and spotted the gap. He took off flying, with Nick Holton right next to him, and the two of them made up at least 20 metres before they were caught. Luckily, Phaphama was right there to pick up the ball and he sprinted off towards the corner at full speed. No one was even close to him as he dotted the ball on the line. The whole team jumped for joy and then breathed a sigh of relief. Finally, they had some points on the board.

Eric glanced over at the Grey staff members and was happy to see that they were taking notes. Andrew looked up and grinned, then raised his hands and clapped for the team. With a rush of confidence, Eric's boys began to play much better than they had in the first half. They competed hard at the breakdowns and ran great attacking lines, but the damage had been done and there was no way they could turn around that points deficit.

By the end of the game, Border had won easily and the Eastern Province team trudged off in disappointment. But the tournament wasn't over, and they recovered quickly to record a narrow victory over Western Province towards the end of the day.

The mood in the bus on the way home was rather subdued. The boys were tired, hungry and far from home, and the excitement of the morning had been replaced by aching muscles and exhaustion.

* * *

At that moment, there was no way for Siya to imagine driving up Cape Road towards Grey Junior School, past the sprawling homes that looked like mansions, the golf driving range and the Mercedes-Benz dealership. But not too long after the end of the tournament, that's exactly what happened.

Siya felt like he was living in a Hollywood movie. Was this really happening? It was too ... perfect. The immaculately mowed lawns, the sprinklers watering the flowers, people walking their dogs or jogging with headphones on along a tree-lined avenue – all of it not even 30 minutes' away from where he had grown up and lived his whole life.

The last few weeks had been surreal, and life-changing. A few days after the team got back from Mossel Bay, Eric had come to visit Siya at his home. He wanted to speak to the boy's grandmother, and his father too, and Siya had been worried that he might have done something wrong and that he was being expelled. In fact, it was the exact opposite. He had been offered a full scholarship to attend Grey Junior School, which included living arrangements in the boarding house, uniform, school books ... all expenses paid. And not just him but Zolani Faku and Phaphama Hoyi as well. All they had to do was play rugby and go to school, which is what they were going to do anyway. It was more than Siya had dreamed possible. He hadn't even known what to say or how to thank anyone who was involved in this process.

After they gratefully accepted the offer, there were a thousand things to organise and plan. The Zwide community and Emsengeni staff met with the parents of the three boys and helped them understand what would be expected of them. The whole community knew what a big opportunity this was. They spoke about weekends, homework, getting the boys to school on time, visiting the school, pocket money and many other details that made the boys feel as if they were going off to live on another planet and not just in a different part of town. But, eventually, all the administration was completed and the boys were ready to leave. Siya said a quiet farewell to his grandmother and to Liyema before the taxi arrived, and then he found himself on the way to his first term at Grey Junior.

If the drive to the school had felt surreal, it was nothing compared to Siya's first impression of Grey High School. It was a feeling he would remember for the rest of his life. The magnificent Edwardian stone buildings, surrounded by emerald-green fields and black wrought-iron fencing, the historic clock tower in the middle, the oak-lined avenue that ran down the middle of the campus ... everything. It was all just ... perfect.

The taxi deposited the three boys on the field just outside the office. They unloaded their simple possessions and looked around in wonder, staring up at the clock tower, which seemed to capture all the history, pride and dignity of the school. The boys were curious and wandered closer towards the narrow, dark doorway at the base of the tower.

'Stop!' They heard a shout from behind them, and looked around to see Andrew Hayidakis calling them over to the junior school entrance.

'We have a long-standing tradition here, boys. You only go through that doorway twice while you are a pupil at this school. Once on your first day of high school and a second time on the day that you leave.'

They listened carefully, determined not to make any mistakes that might jeopardise their places at the school.

'On that day when you enter high school, a matric boy will help you put your tie on, the whole school gathers to sing the "G" – that's our war cry – and then you're one of us.'

Siya nodded, hoping desperately that he would get that honour.

'Follow me,' said Andrew. 'I'll take you to your new home for the next year.'

As they walked out of the school grounds and down the road towards the Warring Lodge hostel, Siya thought back to his home and his family just a short distance away on the other side of Port Elizabeth. They had all gathered to say goodbye to him as the taxi pulled away, and he had tried to tell them it wasn't very far away, but in truth, now that he was here, it felt like a different planet.

Siya had imagined things couldn't get any better than they already were, but when he first saw Warring Lodge in King Georges Road, he began to revise his opinion. It was a large, white double-storey with an English country-house feel to it.

There were balconies running along two sides of the house, upstairs and downstairs, and a big tree in the middle of the garden that provided soft shade, a swimming pool and a braai area round the back.

Between the pool and the main house was a fully decked-out games room with foosball and table tennis tables, and wooden chests full of board games. There was also a computer lab that was painted blue and white, with comfy beanbags, chairs and desktop computers where you could do your homework.

What must this moment have felt like for Siya? How did he absorb it all? How did he get used to the fact that this was all there for him, and that no one was going to take it away? Not many of his dreams had come true in the first decade of his life, and so it was only natural that he would have his guard up for a while. He probably didn't want to get overexcited in case something went wrong, it was all a dream, and he discovered that he wasn't really supposed to be here.

That night, for the first time in his life, Siya slept in a bed and occupied a space that he could really call his own. He was sharing a room with five other Grade 7 boys. They each had their own beds, their own personal drawers to store their things and a hook to hang their school bags on. Just before bedtime on that first night, the housemistress came over with a big pile of clothes that the school was donating to the three boys from Zwide. There were white shorts and a blue rugby jersey for matches, a full tracksuit and slip-slops, not to mention shirts, grey shorts, tie, cap, blazer, socks ... everything that he would need to fit in with the rest of the school and join what felt like one big, happy family.

Lying in bed that night, Siya thought about Liyema at home in Zwide. He wondered if he could feel that Siya was not there, and if he missed him. It was going to be a big change for the little guy, but at least there would be more space in the house, and more food for him to eat now that Siya was being taken care of. A wave of gratitude and relief washed over Siya as he fell asleep. That night, Siya slept more soundly than he ever had in his whole life.

5
■

The Grey

The next few weeks were a whirlwind of growth for the boys from Zwide. Phaphama, Zolani and Siya each had different strengths and weaknesses, and they stuck together as they navigated the strange new world they found themselves in.

Their most urgent need was to improve their English. Barely any isiXhosa was spoken at Grey. Siya, in particular, was struggling to keep up with all the instructions and information that were coming his way. He was hungry to learn as much as he could about the school, but his language skills were holding him back.

The school could see the problem too, and they knew how to handle it. It was decided that the three boys could skip Afrikaans class as they were going to take isiXhosa as a second language, so they focused on remedial English classes every day during Afrikaans period. The teacher assigned to them was Adie Mukheibir, who was the school's academic support coordinator.

'Siya was a little overwhelmed at first,' she remembers. 'He was quiet but you could see he was sussing it all out.'

Every day, Siya, Phaphama and Zolani had extra English

lessons in Mrs Mukheibir's small classroom. It was awkward at first. The pupils and their new teacher struggled to find ways to connect that were helpful. 'I decided that we would use rugby as a language that we could all share,' she says. She set them vocabulary tests around positions and rules, and made them explain things about the game in English. She got the boys to communicate through the medium of sport. From then on, they made rapid progress and Mrs Mukheibir's classroom quickly became a sanctuary and one of Siya's favourite places to hang out.

One day, Mrs Mukheibir remembers, she asked Siya what his favourite thing about Grey Junior was, to which he replied, 'The socks.' She thought she had misunderstood, but Phaphama told her that was exactly what Siya had meant to say. He had never owned a pair of socks before. He had always just worn his badly fitting school shoes on his bare feet. The socks were a great luxury that Siya really appreciated.

On another occasion, the trio were learning the names of animals when it became obvious that they had never seen a wild animal in real life. It seemed wrong that they lived in Africa but had never been given the opportunity to visit a nature reserve. The following weekend, Mrs Mukheibir arranged for the boys to spend the weekend at her house, and took them on a trip to the Seaview Predator Park, west of the city. They drove into the park and stared in wonder at wildebeest, impala, giraffe and crocodile. They visited the enclosure where they saw Nebbie, the dominant male lion in the park, and his two snow-white cubs, Thor and Lily White. They were the first white lions ever born in the Eastern Cape. It was an unforgettable experience for the boys.

Adie Mukheibir became close to all three boys, and they

ended up spending many weekends at her home, becoming part of the family.

It seems likely that those first few months at Grey Junior were a time of healing for Siya. Every day, he felt a little bit more like he belonged. Every day, his worldview expanded. Sometimes he would have felt guilty about what he had left behind. When he looked around the school library, with its thousands of books divided by genre, age group and theme, and then he thought about the Emsengeni library, which was nothing more than a classroom with old workbooks piled up chaotically on shelves, it probably hurt him somewhere deep inside. There was nothing he could do about it at that moment, but maybe one day he could do something for Zwide.

But he never stayed unhappy for long. His dreams were coming true and it made him so happy to be able to call up his grandmother and tell her about everything that was happening in his life. Not just the big things, but also the small ones he hadn't expected. His first trip to the beach with a group of friends. Siya actually burst into tears at the feel of the sand between his toes. Having inspection every morning to check his uniform and his bed-making skills. She laughed when he told her he was already a champion at foosball, how much his tackling had improved now that the fields were grass, and how strange it was that the boarding house was so structured that there was even a time allocated for brushing your teeth.

There was no denying that the discipline of hostel life and the school timetable was good for him. There were boys in his dorm who moaned and groaned about all the rules, but Siya wasn't one of them. After making his way for so long without anyone even noticing what he was doing, the discipline felt to him like freedom and his housemates felt like brothers.

All of the wonderful experiences, the new friends, the thrill of learning, paled in comparison to the one thing he got used to very quickly ... the food. There was so much of it, and it just kept on coming. Breakfasts of eggs, toast, orange juice, porridge ... lunches with meat and salad and potatoes, whole chickens for dinner at Mrs Mukheibir's house, ice cream for dessert, snacks when you felt like it, braais at his friends' houses, cake on someone's birthday ... the list went on and on. His grandmother listened and laughed when he told her how much he was eating. Siya hadn't really known what it was like to feel so full, and sometimes he honestly worried that he was going to explode.

It gave him insight into why his team had not done that well at the Eastern Province trials. It was hard to play on an empty stomach against players who were being fuelled up regularly with nutritious, energy-giving foods. In fact, he was proud of his team for doing so well considering how little they had eaten before that tournament.

When Siya went back home on weekends, he liked to be dropped off wearing his Grey Junior uniform. He naturally assumed that all his old friends and neighbours would be happy for him and proud that one of their own was making it. There were many people who felt that way, but it was by no means everyone. In the years to come, his high-school coach, Dean Carelse, would drop him off after games on a Saturday, and he remembers that 'his two friends didn't want to wear the uniform because it was perceived as "You are too good for us."' They were bullied, but Siya always went in school clothes. He wasn't going to allow anyone to dampen his pride in his school.

So, life was a lot better but of course it wasn't perfect. There was a source of anxiety that was hard to put into words. He was too busy and too excited to stop and wonder what it was, but perhaps if he had done so, he would have realised that his grandmother's health had taken a turn for the worse. There was a weariness in her gaze that hadn't been there before. Walking was becoming difficult, and she spent more time than ever just lying in her bed and resting. 'I washed her, fed her, and walked around with her,' he explained to journalist Angus Powers.

Siya wasn't home very much in 2004, and when he was, he spent a lot of time playing with Liyema, who brought much joy and fun into the Mthembu Street home. Perhaps his grandmother could see that Siya had found a path and that he was going to be all right. Perhaps that finally was enough for her and she felt ready to let go of the daily struggle. 'One day I was in the kitchen and she just dropped,' says Siya. 'I caught her and put her down slowly. I was talking to her but she wouldn't say anything back.'

Siya realised that he needed to get help right away. Even though he hated to leave her alone, he rushed over to the neighbours' house. He remembers: 'They came, and the pastor came and checked, and they said she had passed away.'

Shock. Denial. Panic. Crushing sadness. Siya stood in the impact zone as waves of emotion crashed into him and sent him reeling backwards as if they were actual physical blows. He felt Liyema in his arms, then he was taken away, he was inside the house, then he found himself outside, taking deep gasps of air.

Siya's whole life tumbled around in his brain and he couldn't make sense of any of it. He felt numb and distant. This had all happened so fast, so unexpectedly, and he couldn't process it. 'I was too young to know what had happened.'

That night, finally, he fell asleep and the world, with all its trauma, faded away to nothing.

The next morning the sun came up and the community, who were unbearably experienced at dealing with trauma, lifted him up, held him, and comforted him. The healing hands of time embraced the 12-year-old boy and pointed him in the direction of healing.

Many years later, Siya says, 'I didn't freak out. I didn't cry. I still haven't cried to this day ... which is actually killing me when I think about it.'

Life went on.

His grandmother was buried, Liyema went to live with his biological father, and arrangements were made for Siya to stay with various members of the community on the weekends and during the holidays.

6

■

Rising Through the Ranks

Siya tied the thick white rope around his waist and kicked the tyre downfield until the rope was taut behind him. Then he took a deep breath, waited for the whistle, and exploded into action, sprinting across the field with the heavy black tyre dragging behind him. He pulled up after 70 metres, gasping for breath. Then, as he began to recover, he heard the whistle again, so he turned and raced back. Since he began playing competitively, Siya had been selected at eighth man, combining his strength and speed with his ball-handling skills. But he was still smaller than most of the opposition he played against and he needed to get stronger fast.

The tyres were part of rugby life at Grey High School. They even had individual nicknames, and Siya was pretty certain that he was dragging 'Suzie' around that day. She was the heaviest of them all.

Siya had done well enough at Grey Junior to move into the high school and keep his full scholarship. His easy-going nature and infectious laugh made him popular with his peers and teachers, and his commitment to the school was absolute.

But high-school sports were a significant step up in skill and commitment. Training was at a level that none of the previous stars of the Under-13 'A' had experienced before. There was a big jump in the standard between primary- and high-school rugby: there was more on-field contact, and everyone was dealing with the onset of puberty at different times. Small boys suddenly turned into giants, while some of the big ones barely changed at all. Siya was still small, but he took whatever happened in his stride and kept coming back for more. His dedication to the game was total.

Following the death of his grandmother, the thought must have crystallised in his mind until it felt like a mantra: rugby had saved his life. If he had still been at Emsengeni Primary when his gran died and his world fell apart, then who knows what would have happened to him? Without the game, he would be on a road to nowhere, and he planned to honour the chance he had been given.

Coming into Grade 8 with a full scholarship, Siya threw himself into training with a ferocity and a commitment that were unusual in Under-14 rugby. His new coach was Dean Carelse, a young and passionate teacher who was also eager to make his mark in the world of coaching. Dean dreamed of shaping a team that would go down in Grey history as one of the best the school had produced. He believed that if he got the team right at Under-14 level, then they would be able to stick together until they were 17- and 18-year-olds playing for the Grey High First XV, by which time they would be a formidable unit.

Dean was also Siya's housemaster at Merriway House, where Siya boarded, so their goals were aligned perfectly, and the pair quickly got down to work with a weekly plan that they stuck to religiously.

'Mondays were light sessions,' Dean explains, 'designed to

run out the stiffness and the aches and pains from the weekend games. A little touch rugby, or a quick gym session, maybe
some sprints.'

The hard work happened on Tuesdays. Those were the very
physical training days, with defensive drills and continuity
drills with bags for at least an hour, followed by full-contact
games, either against another team or with a split between
the forwards and the backs.

Wednesdays were video sessions during which the team
watched footage of their previous game, thanks to the efforts
of the school audiovisual club, followed by a short 45-minute
gym session.

Thursdays were about polishing up the team for the weekend.
'I would have seen the video of the opposition during the week,
so I put this into practice,' says Carelse. The team worked on
strategy as a group, and then the backs and forwards split up
again to work on their specific areas of the game.

Friday's schedule was more flexible, depending on the circumstances of the next game. If it was an away game, then the team
would often travel together on a Friday evening; if the game was
at home, then they would watch video of the opposition before
attending the school hockey matches. Training was light on a
Friday, and the focus stayed on the upcoming contest.

It may only have been schoolboy rugby but the preparations on game day felt very similar to what they would be for
any professional team. That's how the Grey coaching staff
approached the game, and how they wanted the boys to start
thinking. On Saturday morning, brunch with the team was
followed by a final team meeting to go over the game plan
one more time. Then there were one-on-one meetings with
the players while the biokineticist and the physiotherapist

arrived and set up. These professionals help the players to manage and understand their bodies and their injuries from week to week.

After a last snack and some water, the players did their final warm-ups and the game began.

And that's what they did, day after day, week after week, all season long. The Under-14s watched every first-team game and were keenly aware of how much the game meant to their school and to its reputation. They knew the history of the school and the great players of the past, and they looked up to the first-team players as if they were celebrities.

For the players on rugby scholarships, there are no illusions about why they are there. If they do well at school and stand out, then the professional game beckons. Scouts from the major unions are reading the results in the newspaper and staying in touch with the school coach, and of course they come to the big games to see the talent for themselves.

To this day, the pressure builds early at Grey, and each team is expected to win. But in 2005, Siya's first year of high school, few people could have predicted that the young man was destined to become a star. He didn't really stand out on the field. The fact of the matter was that, at Under-14 level, Phaphama Hoyi was the guy everyone was watching. His speed and strength made him unstoppable, and he scored over 40 tries in 2005. Siya, by no means the star, was happy just to be on the team and playing.

Every season there were some huge clashes between Grey High School and the top schoolboy teams in the country. Games against Paul Roos, Paarl Gimnasium and Grey College Bloemfontein attracted national interest. Although the first-team clash was the highlight of a visit, those occasions were about more than just rugby. For those big weekend visits, the whole school would set off on a Thursday or Friday, travelling in a fleet of buses like an invading army, and then make camp in the enemy's territory for a weekend of sports, fun and entertainment. The chess team came along, as did debating, tennis and hockey. There were staff lunches, and cocktail parties and a chance to rekindle friendships between staff members and players that stretched back over the years. Siya had never seen anything quite like it.

Many great friendships began on those long trips away from home. The boys spent hours together, telling jokes and laughing, teasing each other, playing tricks and then giving everything for their team-mates and their school out on the field. Those school trips up to Bloemfontein, or down to Paarl and Cape Town, were the first time Siya got to see a world outside Zwide and Port Elizabeth, and it gave him a sense of perspective on his life and on the country.

It was so interesting to see how other schools operated, what their boarding hostels and their school traditions were like, and the boys spent hours discussing the differences between their respective schools. The trips were always great but Siya also loved getting back to the Grey hostel after a weekend away. Merriway House had become his home.

At high school, the boys didn't have to go home for weekends, as they had at junior school. This made things easier for Siya, as he no longer had a permanent home to go back to. He was always getting invited to spend weekends with friends and teachers, and he loved doing that, but sometimes it was also great just to spend quiet time in the hostel where he knew exactly who he was.

One of the best things that happened to Siya in his first year at Grey Junior School was getting to know Nick Holton, who became a full boarder at Grey in Grade 5, a couple of years before Siya arrived. This was the start of an enduring friendship. They had met briefly at the Eastern Province trials in Mossel Bay where Siya was discovered, but their friendship really took off when they lived in the hostel together.

Nick was a popular guy, always ready with a joke and a story, and people naturally gravitated to him. For someone so young, he was at ease with who he was, and that made everyone else relax too. He was a natural, charismatic leader and he and Siya really hit it off. They were both crazy about sports, stayed in the hostel together, played on the same team, and were in the same class.

Siya struggled badly in his first two terms at school and Nick took it upon himself to see how he could help. He began looking over Siya's homework before he handed it in, in exchange for isiXhosa lessons, and it really paid off. Siya never forgot this commitment from his friend.

Nick's parents lived in Knysna, but they often used to drive to Port Elizabeth to watch the big games. They grew fond of Siya and could see how strong the friendship was between the two boys. They began inviting Siya to spend holidays with them in Knysna, and he enjoyed many magical days and nights with the Holton family on the Garden Route. At school on the weekends when they were by themselves, Nick became curious about Siya's life in Zwide, and sometimes the two of them would take a taxi to Zwide together to hang out and watch the African Bombers play and meet Siya's friends from the township.

In a totally natural way, the endless conversations with Nick and his family did as much for Siya's English as the extra lessons with Mrs Mukheibir. His English had improved so rapidly in Grade 7 that the new people he met at high school the following year would never have guessed that he had barely been able to speak the language a year earlier.

Weekends in Zwide were difficult now. Slowly, he began to lose touch with many of the people and places that had formed the backdrop of his first decade. He rarely saw either of his parents in those years, and much as he was doing at Grey, his old friends from Emsengeni Primary were growing up, moving on, and living their own lives.

He spent some time at the home of Anele Pamba, who was an administrator at the Eastern Province Rugby Union and who saw Siya's potential. But the one place where he could always go to reconnect was at Dan Qeqe Stadium with the African Bombers. The club welcomed Siya with open arms whenever he was back in Zwide and provided him with the sense of belonging that was so important to him. Whenever there was time and an opportunity, Siya would jump at the chance to pull on an African Bombers jersey and play his heart out for his old club, even though this was against Grey rules.

But he knew that Eric and the players in the team expected it from him. He didn't want to give the impression that he was too important to play for the Bombers, so he just played the games and didn't mention it to anyone when he got back to school.

Those games for the Bombers taught Siya how to stay out of trouble on the field. Physically, he was a lot smaller than many of his opponents, and he couldn't afford to arrive back at school with bumps and bruises that he would have to explain. It made him think tactically about how to look after himself, to learn how to read the game, to respond early to situations, and to improve his support play. 'Because he was small for his age group, he couldn't bully people, or make the big tackles, or the big runs,' says Dean Carelse, 'so he had to learn how to be streetwise.' Ultimately, it made Siya into a well-rounded team player with a great set of skills that he could use to his advantage.

Siya played eighth man from Under-13 to Under-16 level, both for Grey High and when he was representing Eastern Province. The coach moved him to number 7 when he was in Grades 11 and 12, 'and he bounced between numbers 7 and 8 when he played Craven Week and SA Schools,' says Carelse. The versatility and adaptability that came with switching positions was just one more aspect that made him so valuable to whatever team he was playing in.

Many of his friends at Grey had become dedicated 'gym bunnies' and they were constantly encouraging Siya to join them for a workout in the school gym, but it wasn't something that particularly interested him. He had also been told by one of the school doctors that he was still growing naturally and that he shouldn't be lifting weights at this stage of his development. Siya was relieved to not have to do gym, and he was confident that he would have a growth spurt at some time in the future.

His lack of stature just made him work harder.

One of the most exciting things that happened at Grey High was the rare occasions when the Springboks came to train on the school fields. It didn't happen very often, but occasionally the team had a game scheduled in Port Elizabeth and the whole squad would arrive for a training session. One year, it was the Springbok squad that included legendary players like captain John Smit, Victor Matfield, Bobby Skinstad and

Siya's personal hero, Schalk Burger. For Siya to see these players in real life, on the very same fields where he played, was an awesome experience. It made them into real people, and it made his own dreams of wearing the green and gold that much more real. Years later, he recalled that experience and told *City Press*: 'I remember my heart became so hot and I wanted to burst from excitement. I wasn't aware of anything around me, just the Springboks. From the first time I picked up a rugby ball and ran with it, I wanted to wear that green jersey. And on that day, I really started to believe I could.'

Confidence was everything in those first few years of high school, and the coach could see that Siya's was growing every week, both on and off the pitch. He had never learned to swim but he grew sick and tired of watching from the side of the swimming pool as the other boys trained. How hard could it be, really? So, one afternoon, when everyone else was in the pool, he just stood up, gathered his courage, and jumped into the water. Courage and fearlessness are powerful weapons but they are no match for the law of gravity, and the water-polo pool had no shallow end. Siya immediately sank to the bottom. Luckily, his friends and his team-mates were all around him and they jumped into action, diving down to the bottom of the pool and raising him up to the surface.

They dragged Siya out of the pool, coughing and spluttering. After the shock wore off and everyone realised that he was okay, the shock turned to amusement. Siya just laughed it off. His bravery was an asset on the rugby field, but that didn't mean he could swim just because he really wanted to.

At the end of 2007, word reached Siya that his mother had given birth to another baby, a girl called Liphelo. He was glad for her, but at the same time he couldn't help wondering if she would be able to take care of the baby. He also worried a lot about Liyema, the half-brother who had lived with him and his grandmother. He had lost touch with Liyema since the boy's father took him away after his gran's death, and he had no idea where he was living.

But he didn't have a lot of time to worry about anything. Life was getting busier and busier, the schoolwork was getting harder and harder, and everyone was telling him that it was only a matter of time before he made it into the Grey first team.

Grade 10 was the year that Siya first came to the attention of the Springbok management. The South African Rugby Union (SARU) doesn't monitor players before they play at Under-16 level, as they are still growing and changing too fast. 'Earlier than that, the guys are not physically developed yet,' says Herman Masimla, the manager of Elite Player Development programmes for SARU.

Siya had performed well and worked hard all season and he was rewarded with an invitation to the Under-16 Grant Khomo Week, where he played some brilliant rugby for Eastern Province. This led to an invitation to join SARU's Elite Squad for 2007. It was a great honour and a vote of confidence in his ability. 'It means a lot to a player to get that recognition, over and above from the union,' says Masimla.

Between 60 and 80 players from all over the country come together for a week in a national training camp. This is the first chance for SARU to do a full skills assessment and a physical and medical assessment, to check diet and conditioning, and to build a bit of a social profile on the most promising young players in the country. Those who have been selected don't play competitive matches at this point, but attending the camp represents a tremendous endorsement for a young player. All the information gathered on the players is shared with them and their school in order to help push their careers in the right direction. Siya left the training camp with a new sense of purpose and a belief that if he did everything right, he could have a career as a professional rugby player.

* * *

In Siya's life, tragedy often seemed to come along at the exact moment when things were going really well for him. This had happened with his grandmother, and it had made him wary of ever feeling too comfortable. It was around this time, when he was really finding himself at Grey High School, that he heard the news that his mother had passed away in Zwide. He was stunned. To lose his grandmother had been the worst thing that ever happened to him; to lose his mother as well was too much to take. The whole school rallied around and supported him to help him get through the ordeal, but there was no denying that the loss of his mother would leave permanent scars on his life.

He would never have the relationship with Phakama that he had dreamed about. He would always wonder what their life together could have been like, and he would never know. At the funeral, he saw Liyema and Liphelo for one last time before they disappeared back into the township. It was all too much to handle, and he felt the weight of expectations settle heavily on his shoulders. He was the one who had made it out, and perhaps his success could drag a whole family out of poverty.

* * *

56

The death of his mother had a profound impact on Siya's life, but slowly he recovered and was able to focus on moving forward. Things began looking up again in the second half of 2007, not only for Siya himself but for South African rugby as a whole. In September of that year, the national team travelled to France for the Rugby World Cup and the rhythm of life at Grey shifted so that everyone could watch the tournament.

The Springboks had been drawn in Group A alongside England, Samoa, Tonga and the United States, but it was only England who were considered to be any kind of threat to the Springboks' progress into the knockout stages. The biggest game of Group A took place at the Stade de France, in Paris, on 14 September, and South Africa sent out a clear message to the rest of the world that they were the team to beat that year.

The Springboks' performance against England was simply awe-inspiring in every department. They scored three tries, three conversions and five out of five penalties, with no answer from the defending champions, who saw an eight-game winning streak come to an end. An early try in the sixth minute from Juan Smith set the tone for the game, and Fourie du Preez was explosive at scrumhalf, earning himself the man-of-the-match award.

Dean Carelse watched the game with his players, and he kept drawing their attention to the breakdowns, where the Springboks were dominant. They ended up stealing the ball nine times at the breakdown and running away with the game. It was a superb performance and it gave the Boks a large dose of confidence. They cruised through the rest of their group matches, then into the quarter-finals, where they dispatched Fiji by 37 points to 20, before easily beating Argentina by 37 to 13 in the semi-finals.

People were saying this was one of the best South African teams of all time, and it wasn't hard to see why. With John Smit as the inspirational captain, Bryan Habana flying down the wing, and individual stars such as Victor Matfield, Bakkies Botha and Fourie du Preez leading the charge, the whole nation quickly got behind the team and their cunning coach, Jake White.

After the embarrassing defeat to the Boks in their opening game, England recovered well and managed to win their way through to the final for a rematch. Back at the Stade de France for the World Cup final, the Springboks maintained their discipline and thwarted the English team at every turn. England's star kicker, Jonny Wilkinson, was off his usually excellent game and he missed two drop kicks at crucial moments. England trailed by 9 points to 3 at the break, but they started the second half with a flourish that saw winger Mark Cueto go over for a try. But, after a long look at it, the TV match official ruled that Cueto had been in touch when he scored and cancelled the try. South Africa kept up the pressure with a solid kicking display from Percy Montgomery and Francois Steyn and led 15–6 when the final whistle blew.

There were uproarious celebrations back at Grey High School. The Springboks were world champions for the second time, and South African rugby was once again the benchmark against which all other countries would be judged. Siya was delighted. He knew by this point that he wanted nothing more than to be a professional rugby player and to test himself against the stars that he watched on television week in and week out.

There was a strong possibility that he would be playing first-team rugby during the coming season. This would be the opportunity to put all his dreams to the test.

7
■

The First XV

Not only was 2008 an important year for Siya, but it was also a big one for rugby at Grey High School in general. Dean Carelse was promoted to the position of first-team coach. His plan to create a cohesive, well-drilled group of players who knew each other intimately had worked to perfection. All they had to do was work hard, prepare for the big games, and execute – and that's exactly what they did.

The growth spurt that Siya had longed for finally arrived when he was in Grade 11. He left the school during the Christmas holidays as one of the boys and came back a man. The transformation was so remarkable that it was almost hard to believe he was the same guy. The skills he had learned to avoid trouble and to play for the team wherever he was needed were now complemented by a massive frame of muscle and power. He had learned how to break tackles, to be strong over the ball in the rucks, and to link up easily with the back-line, and now it was his turn to step into the limelight. He seized it with both hands.

The 2008 rugby season was one of the greatest seasons of schoolboy rugby that Grey High School had ever produced. If it hadn't been for one heartbreaking loss, the Grey High team would have remained unbeaten all season for the first time in 30 years. They averaged almost 40 points a game, despite the fact that 60 per cent of their matches were played away.

The team was captained by Bonakele Bethe, known affectionately as 'Bones'. He was the first black captain in the school's history, and he wore the powder-blue school jersey with pride and passion and was a great inspiration for his team-mates. For most of the season, Grey High School was ranked top in the country, and it was no surprise when 13 players in the squad were awarded Eastern Province colours.

The season kicked off on a high note with a 59–0 win over Hudson Park, followed by a clean sweep at the Grey Rugby Festival, against Hilton, Michaelhouse and Helpmekaar. From there the team really started picking up winning momentum. They steamrollered Graeme College, then beat Rondebosch, SACS and Pretoria Boys at the Queen's Rugby Festival.

After this run of victories came Craven Week, which was an annual highlight on the schoolboy rugby calendar. The best teams in the country gathered for a week to showcase their talent, but the Eastern Province side struggled. 'Our EP team didn't do that well,' Siya told the *Algoa Sun*. 'However, we always tried to do the most we could when we had the ball.' Siya's determination was rewarded after the tournament when he heard that he had been selected for the SA Schools side, alongside his team-mate Chuma Faas, who said he 'was shocked and surprised – lost for words – when I heard I was chosen'.

It was another major milestone on Siya's career path, and another endorsement of his talent. Besides Kolisi and Faas, there were a few more selections from Grey High School: Phaphama Hoyi made the SA Academy side, while Kurt Coleman, Sikhokele Blom and Siyanda Mangaliso all made the Southern Regional side.

Quite a few of the Grey first-team players picked up minor niggles during the 2008 Craven Week, which they had to manage in training, but they were able to overcome the problems and deliver a devastating blow just a week later to their biggest rivals, Paul Roos Gimnasium, whom they beat 41–16 away. For Siya, this was probably the biggest game of his life to date. He'd never seen crowds like this at a match and the noise was deafening. It seemed that the whole of Stellenbosch had turned out to watch the game, but the players were determined not to be overwhelmed. They focused on the little things, on putting together long passages of unbroken play and building momentum, and it paid off. By half-time they were up by 31 points to 11, thanks to a pair of tries from Hayden de Villiers and another by Sikhokele Blom. The Paul Roos crowd was stunned into silence by the quality of Grey's teamwork.

In the second half, an illegal tackle from Hayden de Villiers led to a yellow card and the team were forced to defend with only 14 players, but they got through it. Then more points went up on the board through tries from Craig Millson and Carl van Niekerk, and some perfect kicking off the boot of Kurt Coleman. Thanks to an all-round team effort and a focus on getting the basics right, the mighty Paul Roos had been humbled. It was at that point in the season that the website Rugby365.com declared Grey High to be the number-one schoolboy team in the country.

The trip home for the school convoy was a non-stop celebration.

The victories kept coming – over Dale College, Queen's College and DF Malherbe – but the biggest hurdle of the season was still ahead. Grey College, their rivals from Bloemfontein, was the one team Grey High were worried about, but spirits were high as the whole school left in a fleet of buses to make the long trip north to the Free State.

If the game against Paul Roos had been a running battle, then this game was trench warfare. Both teams dug in and refused to give an inch. With ten minutes to go, Grey College were leading by five points. In desperation, Bones Bethe and his players sent wave after attacking wave towards the try line, only to be repelled over and over again. It was agonising to watch, and it was almost a relief when the final whistle blew. They had lost 17–22, and the disappointment was intense, but at the same time, Grey High knew they had given their all and provided a thrilling game of rugby for the spectators.

After that defeat, the team bounced back quickly and won their last two games convincingly to record a historic season.

One of the strangest incidents of the 2008 season took place during the big away game against Daniel Pienaar Technical High School in Uitenhage. Daniel Pienaar always put a quality team on the field, and crowds from all over the area would gather to watch the pride of Uitenhage take on their 'big-name' rivals from the coast. These games drew some of the most intense and passionate spectators in the country, and often there were groups of former players, or the parents and siblings of the players, who were out to make a big day of it, drinking and partying, talking about school, and reminiscing about the big games that they had played in.

It was a close game, but Grey High were up by 20 points to 9 as the second half began. Siya and the rest of the pack were jogging up to the halfway line for a line-out when he heard someone shout his name. He turned to look and saw a spectator running straight at him. At the last second, the guy swerved away from Siya but went straight into the nationally acclaimed referee, Philip Bosch. He hit him in the small of the back and Bosch went down hard. There was absolute chaos. A couple of the players jumped on the drunken spectator, while others attended to the injured referee and the crowd erupted in dismay.

A few moments later, the man who had charged the ref identified his group of friends, and they admitted that it was the result of a stupid, drunken bet. When the press arrived, it turned into a big incident and there was much finger-pointing and indignation about the extremely competitive nature of these schoolboy rugby events. Eventually it blew over, without schoolboy rugby changing at all.

Off the playing field, things were also going well for Siya. His friendships at the school had blossomed and he was feeling increasingly secure in who he was and in his sense of belonging. One of his best friends was a boy called Tyron Coomer, and Siya spent a lot of time at his home in Wilderness when they weren't at school. In his Grade 11 year, Tyron's mother, Heather, raised enough money to take the boys on a short European tour during the summer holidays. It was just another example of how he had been embraced by the Grey High School community, and of how people would go out of their way, time and time again, to do things for him. There was just something in the way that Siya handled himself in the world, from his attitude and his work ethic to his ready smile and his sense of gratitude, that made people respond to him.

But the European trip did force Siya to make some decisions.

The trip was scheduled for the Easter holidays and coincided with one of the big school rugby festivals. Siya was conflicted and afraid to tell his coach that he wouldn't be there. He waited until the last minute but then decided that the trip was too big an opportunity to pass up. Rugby would still be there when he got back.

Travelling around Europe with a few of his best friends for a few weeks was a defining moment for Siya. It had been less than five years since the death of his grandmother, when his future had looked anything but certain, and he was deeply aware of how lucky he had been.

It wasn't only the other parents who were generous with Siya. The school also realised how unfair it was for a boy to go on tour and have to rely on his friends and team-mates for pocket money. They organised to give Siya small amounts of cash to take with him on tour, so that he wouldn't feel like he was a burden on the other players. It was just one more small, generous gesture that went a long way towards normalising his situation.

The year 2008 was when Siya really came out of his shell and started to believe that he had a future in the game. He had always hoped it would be so; now he knew it. Being selected for Eastern Province, then making it into the SA Schools team, was just the kind of proof he needed that he was in the right place at the right time. He knew that there were scouts watching him play, and he was surprised and amused when gifts started arriving from the various provincial rugby unions. Gum guards, scrum caps, supplements ... they were delivered to the hostel on a weekly basis, but Siya didn't want or need any of it, and he was happy to give it all away. But he took the interest as a real sign that he was doing something right.

* * *

By the time Siya came to the end of Grade 11, he knew that his future was intimately tied to rugby. All the signs were there. He felt the need to lay down a marker and commit himself to the game and to secure his future for when school ended.

It's difficult to know when the Cheetahs first became aware of Siya's potential. It's possible that Greg Miller, who was the Under-15 coach in 2009 and had a good relationship with the Free State franchise, alerted them. One thing is clear, though: once they spotted him, they became determined that he would become one of them. 'The Cheetahs began courting Siya, offering him a contract in the region of R300 000 a year and full medical,' says Dean Carelse, 'but Siya had always dreamed of playing for Western Province.' His idol was Schalk Burger and he could think of nothing better than to play on the same team as Schalk. Nevertheless, a concrete offer was hard to turn down, and he accepted it.

As Siya was only 17 at the time this all happened, the contract was future-dated to kick in when he turned 18. Dean Carelse was away on a Jake White coaching course at the time. By the time he found out about it, the deal was done and Siya was destined to move to the Cheetahs after he finished school. Dean tried to make the best of it, telling *SA Rugby* magazine, 'The junior structures in place in the Free State are absolutely top-notch.' Privately, though, Carelse was upset that the Free State franchise had signed his star player while he was still in Grade 11. 'They somehow convinced him that they were the only union who would be interested in him,' but it was too late to do anything about it.

By 2009, when Siya was in his final year of high school, his reputation as a future star had spread far and wide. It wasn't unusual for him to be called over by a parent from the school who wanted to take a picture with him, just in case he became a Springbok one day. He knew that people were talking about him and watching his every move, but it didn't really worry him. He was just going to be himself and do what he had always done. That seemed to be working fine. Which is not to say that Siya was always on his best behaviour. He liked to have fun just like everyone else.

Each of the first-team players was assigned a 'newpot' – a Grade 8 student who was responsible for doing their chores and generally looking after them. Siya's newpot was Nick Beswick, who worshipped the ground that Siya walked on: 'One night he and his two roommates wanted to go out', Nick remembers, 'which was against school rules, so he asked me to sleep in his bed and pretend to be him, in case any of the hostel masters showed up. Sure enough, at around 2 am one of the masters arrived, armed with a torch. I buried my head beneath the duvet, like Siya usually did, and in my deepest voice shouted, "We're all here. Please leave!"'

* * *

As his final year at Grey began, Siya was grateful and delighted to be named as a prefect. This was one of the highest honours that a student could receive, and Siya took it very seriously. He wasn't just any prefect either; he was put in charge of the juniors, and he made sure that they knew what was expected of them and how they should adapt to life at high school.

Siya was beloved by the junior students. They were happy to do whatever he asked of them, and they followed him around the school whenever they had free time. Watching them making their way into high school took Siya back to his early days and reminded him how much he had grown and changed.

Unfortunately, the gap between Siya's life at Grey High School and his life in Zwide kept widening, and there were fewer and fewer reasons for him to go back to the township. It worried him, but he was determined to keep the connection alive.

Yet there were occasions when being back in Zwide became too much for Siya to handle. Dean Carelse recalls how 'Siya would sometimes phone me, late at night, and just say, "Sir, I need to be fetched."' So, the coach would get in his car, drive to Zwide, and take Siya back to the hostel. 'He wouldn't discuss it afterwards,' says Carelse, but it was clear that the hostel was more of a home to Siya than anywhere else.

During his final year at the school, the team came up with an idea that Siya loved. Before a big home game, the school would send a bus to Zwide, gather up some rugby fans, and bring them back to the school to watch the first team play and experience the atmosphere of a home game at Grey.

Port Elizabeth is a charming and tranquil place, but if you're looking for excitement on a Saturday afternoon, your options are limited. That's one of the reasons why there are such crowds at Grey High home games. Many people in the city have some kind of connection to the school and they come together on a Saturday to renew those bonds and show their support.

The bus full of supporters from Zwide would join the throngs of fans as they gathered three, four and five deep around the field. The students would be in full uniform, lined up underneath the clock tower with their arms around each other, belting out war cries and firing up their team. It was always an unbelievable scene, and the fans from Zwide made the most of it.

On the field, the 2009 season was a lot more difficult than the previous one. The team were scheduled to play most of their big games away from home, in addition to a demanding Under-18 provincial schedule. They were stretched thin and were forced to rely on more than 31 players through the season in order to deal with all the injuries.

Many of the stars from the previous season's squad had taken up positions in the provincial unions. Hayden de Villiers and Kurt Coleman had gone to Western Province, Chuma Faas and Sisa Mafu were with the Lions, and the list went on … Siya was also pleased to see that some of his former team-mates had picked the Free State Rugby Union, which he would be joining the following year.

The first game of the season was a disappointing loss by a single point away to Marlow, but the team bounced back and pummelled Clifton by 84 points to nil. They then began a winning streak of five games before losing narrowly to Bishops in Cape Town. Siya had a few breakout moments in the early part of the season. Against Dale College, he collected the ball on his own 22-metre line, broke numerous tackles, and ran nearly the full length of the field before offloading to winger Craig Millson to score. Against Graeme College he combined beautifully with Siyanda Mangaliso as they switched the ball back and forth before Siya went over the line. Kurt Coleman and Phaphama Hoyi also put in some brilliant performances during the early part of the season.

After that tour, all eyes turned to the upcoming home match against Paul Roos. It had been a big deal for Grey High to beat

Paul Roos 41–16 the previous year, and everyone knew that the team from Stellenbosch would be out for revenge. But the weeks leading up to the match were hectic, including two sets of Craven Week trials, and the players were feeling run-down.

When Siya returned to Zwide the weekend before the big game, he was keeping a guilty secret from his coach. But he felt he had no choice. The African Bombers were scheduled to play against Spring Rose at the Dan Qeqe Stadium, and he had assured the team that he would be there for them. Out on the pitch that afternoon, the game was as intense and passionate as any Siya had ever played in. He was up against Solly Tyibilika, one of the toughest men in the game, and Siya was feeling it every time he was tackled.

Late in the second half, he drifted out wide and joined the line, then gathered a pass to make five metres before a crunching tackle saw him bundled into the corner. Siya felt his foot land awkwardly and a searing pain rush up from his ankle. The pain was bad, but it was nothing compared to the fear of what would happen when he told Coach Carelse back at school. Siya hobbled off and wrapped the ankle in ice, but it was too late. The damage was done.

At school on Monday morning, he gathered his courage and told the coach that he'd been playing soccer in the street when he hurt himself, but that he was sure he'd be okay. 'The ankle was so bad that he couldn't walk,' said Carelse, 'and when we took him off to the doctor, he was told there was a chance he would never play again.'

Siya was crushed. This was not the way it was supposed to happen, but he knew his body and was certain that he would recover. He just needed a little time. He embarked on an intensive rehab programme in the days leading up to the Paul Roos visit, and the ankle responded positively. When Siya began insisting that the ankle was fine, the medical team went off and did a few scans, but the doctor decided that he was nowhere near ready to play.

Siya's mood darkened the day before the match when the buses from Paul Roos rolled into the Grey High School grounds. He tried to convince the coaching staff that he was fine, and that he could play, but they would not budge. Siya tried to resign himself to watching from the sidelines.

An hour before the game was due to start, the heavens opened and soaked the playing field. When the game kicked off, the playing surface was slippery and muddy, and disaster struck twice in the first 15 minutes. Both of the Grey High wingers were injured and had to be taken off. Everything seemed to be going against the team, but they stuck to their game plan with dogged determination, and at the break the sides were level at ten points apiece. Once more, Siya begged the coach to let him play, but Dean Carelse was having none of it.

With ten minutes to go, the score was still level at 13–13, and Siya felt like he was losing his mind. This was his kind of game; there were weaknesses in the Paul Roos midfield and he knew that was his channel. He was big enough and strong enough now to make it very difficult for the other teams to take him out when he had the ball, and he would be breaking the advantage line regularly in a game like this. This was the kind of rugby he was born to play. Siya made a hasty decision that he could not miss this game, so he charged off to the hostel, hauled out his rugby kit, and got dressed. There was no way that the coach could deny him when he saw Siya in the powder-blue jersey.

As he jogged back towards the field, the home spectators

spotted him and a cheer went up around the ground. They knew this would be a turning point.

'Put me in, coach,' shouted Siya as he got back onto the touchline. 'I'll score you tries!'

Dean Carelse looked him up and down and heard the crowd roaring, 'Si-ya, Si-ya, Si-ya!' He knew exactly what his star player could achieve in these circumstances, but he also knew what kind of a career Siya could enjoy when he left school. He couldn't risk it all for one schoolboy game. It was agonising. 'But the fact is,' says Carelse, 'I didn't want to be the coach who ruined a young boy's career. I couldn't do it, even though I knew we would have won.'

The clock ticked down with Siya still waiting on the sidelines. The Grey fullback tried to clear from behind the try line but fluffed his kick. The Paul Roos forwards were on it like a pack of wolves and bundled the ball back over the line for a try. All the fight went out of Siya's eyes; he couldn't even look at his coach. He marched back up to the hostel in a fury and changed out of his kit as he heard the whistle to signal the end of the game.

Deep down inside, he admired the coach for sticking to his guns in the face of all that pressure, but he was furious that he hadn't been allowed to play, and ashamed that he had gotten himself injured before such a big game. There was a reason he had won the award for Best Team Player that year; everything he did, he did for the team. Yet in the one game where it really mattered, this happened!

It took him a few weeks before he was able to look Dean Carelse in the eye and speak to him without feeling a sense of anger and resentment. Siya wasn't going to let that kind of thing happen again.

Yet, despite the disappointment of losing to Grey's rivals, there were plenty of encouraging signs that convinced Siya his career was on the right track, and nothing was bigger than being selected again for the SA Schools team. This was the highest honour in schoolboy rugby and was the result of a good performance at Craven Week.

Siya had been chosen as a replacement player when he was in Grade 11, and then in the starting lineup during Grade 12. It meant the world to him to line up alongside the best young players in the country, guys like Patrick Lambie and Bongi Mbonambi whom he had been playing against for years in school tournaments around the country. He had seen how good these guys were and he was honoured to be counted among them in a team that had been selected to play against Italy in Kimberley later that year.

That year, Craven Week had been a whirlwind. There was a buzz around Siya from the moment he got there. The word had spread to all the coaches that there was an intriguing new player from the Eastern Cape, but their enthusiasm at watching him play turned to frustration when they heard he had already signed for the Cheetahs.

Meanwhile, Siya was having second thoughts about moving to Bloemfontein. When he had signed, his confidence had been at a low point and he had been led to believe that this was going to be the only offer he would get. But, in his heart, he had always been a Western Province and Stormers fan, mainly because of his admiration for Schalk Burger, and that had never changed.

That week, Siya felt like he was living under a microscope. A lot of people were watching very closely to see if he would be able to convert all his potential. One of the people monitoring his career closely was Hilton Houghton, a manager-agent from Cape Town who was in the process of launching his own agency, the Union Sports Group.

Hilton was interested in a number of players, in particular Siyabonga 'Scarra' Ntubeni and Siya Kolisi. He knew that Kolisi had already been signed, but something told him that it would be a good idea to just keep the door open. He also believed that Siya would benefit from making the leap from schoolboy to professional with someone like Scarra by his side. They were from the same area, they had taken similar paths to the top, and they were likely to face many of the same challenges in the professional game.

The CEO of the Western Province Rugby Institute (WPRI), Jacques Hanekom, had also been at Craven Week that year, and he was on the lookout for a hooker for Western Province. He was having doubts about one of the hookers in the current setup and he needed to have options. When he saw Scarra Ntubeni playing during Craven Week, he knew that his prayers had been answered.

Hilton heard the news about Scarra, and he asked Jacques Hanekom if he would be interested in taking Siya Kolisi down to Province as well. 'Who wouldn't be interested?' says Jacques. 'But I knew that he was signed.' But when Jacques heard that Siya was a Province fan, he made it clear that he would be very welcome to join the WPRI, which had been launched in 2007 to introduce younger players to the rigours of the modern game.

Hilton knew this was his chance, so he sat down with Siya and made it clear that he would like to represent him, and to get him a deal to move to Cape Town despite his contract with the Cheetahs. Hilton set to work and stumbled on a valuable piece of information: Siya had signed the contract with the Cheetahs when he was under 18 and had not obtained consent from a parent or guardian. The contract had been forward-dated to the time that he turned 18. Hilton was certain that this contract was not legally binding, and that he could nego-tiate a much better deal for his new star player. And that's what he did.

Siya returned to Grey High after Craven Week feeling more settled and sure about his future than ever before. Everything had gone according to plan and he knew for certain what his next move would be: a year in Stellenbosch at the WPRI. He would no longer have the protective blanket that Grey High School had thrown over him, which had allowed him to grow and find himself, free of any financial worries. He had always known that he didn't have the luxury of a gap year or an expen-sive education at a top university. He needed to make a plan of his own and he had gone ahead and done exactly that.

The last few months of high school were full of mixed emotions for Siya and the class of 2009. They worked hard preparing for their final exams, and spent hours planning end-of-year parties and socials, saying goodbye to teachers, and promising to stay in touch with each other for life. Then, one day, it was all over and the boys walked back out through the revered arch in the clock tower for the first time since they had walked in five years earlier.

Siya Kolisi's life was fundamentally shaped by his time at Grey High School. It is safe to say that no other institution would have quite the same influence.

Part 2

8
■

The Transition

Back in Zwide after the end of matric, Siya spent some time living at the home of rugby administrator Anele Pamba, but he found it hard to settle. His shoulder had started to ache on cold nights, and he missed his friends, the school routine and the life he had carefully constructed at Grey High School.

Siya had been looking forward to the end of matric exams and all the celebrations that went along with it. In those first few weeks after school, everyone had partied like crazy and sworn lifelong friendship. But that activity had died down considerably, and now he was just back in Zwide, killing time until the next phase of his journey began.

One night there was a dangerous encounter in the dark with a guy carrying a knife, which shook Siya badly. It's not clear exactly what happened – it was dark and the incident happened so fast – but Siya's commercial agent, Kendra Houghton (the wife of his new agent, Hilton Houghton), thinks that 'he was kitted out in his rugby gear and he actually got stabbed because there were some people who were jealous of him'.

Siya was carrying an old shoulder injury, but the mugging made it a lot worse, and he began to worry that he wouldn't be fit enough to make the Under-19 Western Province team in six months' time. This was the next step on the journey to the pros for the 50 boys who were enrolled at the WPRI. By the end of the programme only half of those players would be selected for Western Province.

Siya called Hilton and Kendra and told them what had happened and about the pain he had in his shoulder. Kendra remembers how, every time she saw him after a trip to Zwide in those days, 'When Siya left he was one person, when he came back he was different.' She decided it was time to make some decisive moves in Siya's career. After all, the situation with signing for the Cheetahs, then backing out and moving to Western Province, had not been an ideal start to a professional career. It was time to safeguard the vulnerable young player they were investing in.

Union Sports Group had signed two players from the Eastern Cape for the WPRI, so they invited both of them to come down early to Cape Town and stay with them until the training began. Siya was delighted at the idea and gratefully accepted, as did the other player, Scarra Ntubeni. They didn't know each other well, but Siya had seen Scarra at Craven Week and had been impressed. Although they were both from the Eastern Cape, Scarra had left Dale College and gone on to King Edward VII School in Johannesburg on a scholarship, so their paths hadn't crossed much.

Siya spent the next few days packing up his life, saying goodbye to friends and family, and visiting Grey High School one last time to thank the teachers and coaching staff for everything they had done for him. Then he set off on a plane to Cape Town, excited to find out what the future held for him.

After arriving in Cape Town, the two young men were taken

into Kendra and Hilton's home and made to feel completely welcome. Kendra remembers how she used to cook for Siya and Scarra, but radically underestimated how much the two of them could eat. 'Once when we served up the meal, Siya took the whole chicken and put it on his plate,' she says, laughing.

Like all 18-year-olds newly graduated from school, they took some time to get used to the fact that there were no more rules and curfews and schedules to follow. They were responsible for their own time now. In those first few weeks and months, in a new town far away from home, Scarra and Siya became firm friends. Two warriors on the same journey, helping one another along the way.

There was plenty happening in Cape Town, and they soaked it all up. Nick Holton and a few other school friends were enrolled at UCT and were slowly arriving to set themselves up. That December, there were plenty of braais and parties to attend, as well as long days at the beach, and long nights enjoying the city's famous nightlife.

In early December 2009, Hilton took Siya out to Stellenbosch for the first time in order to see the WPRI facilities and meet with Johan van Wyk, the head of Performance and Medical, and the medical team who were consulting on Siya's sore shoulder. They ran a series of tests on him and determined that there was a problem that needed to be addressed. Rehab would help but it wasn't going to be a long-term solution. Siya needed Latarjet surgery, a procedure developed by a French surgeon to treat shoulder injuries, and the sooner it happened, the better. Siya was a little surprised that surgery was required, but he trusted the team around him. So, only a few weeks before he turned professional, he found himself in hospital, undergoing surgery, and then beginning the process of rehab.

At that time, the protocol after Latarjet surgery was that players would be out for between 16 and 24 weeks, depending on the extent of the surgery. '[Orthopaedic surgeon] Joe de Beer changed it to 12 to 16 weeks,' Johan van Wyk remembers, 'but Siya was back on the playing field after only ten weeks. Some other guys who had the same op at the same time were still wearing a sling.' Former WPRI head coach Steph Nel agrees, and remembers that 'the amazing thing about Siya is that one week after surgery, his arm was still in a sling and he was out there running around the track. The physio asked, "Why are you doing this?" and he told him straight, "This is my one opportunity in life."'

There was a collective sigh of relief when his body responded so well to the surgery and the rehab.

The first few weeks of 2010, in Stellenbosch and living on the university campus, reminded Siya of what it had been like when he started at Grey Junior in 2004. Back then, the contrast between Zwide and Grey was jarring, and this would have felt similar. In the centre of town, the wide streets lined with oak trees gave way to formal white buildings cloaked with history and tradition. Stellenbosch was, and still is, a shining jewel of a town – polished, sophisticated and welcoming to young people who come from all over the country to attend its prestigious university. At the same time, there are informal settlements such as Kayamandi, Klapmuts and Langrug, just a few kilometres away, where people face daily desperation, sadness and poverty.

If you were to visit the WPRI today, you'd see an institute with world-class facilities, anti-gravity training devices, and a sense of style and design that is more like a five-star hotel than a sporting academy. But in the early years, the

Institute did not have its own premises, and was instead run as part of Stellenbosch University. The players shared dorm rooms, showers and canteens with all the other varsity students. There were good-food days and bad-food days. They had to compete for time in the gym and were often chased off the rugby fields to make way for the Maties, the official university team that was the pride and the joy of all rugby fans in the area. Maties rugby was soaked in tradition, and that team didn't exactly take kindly to the presence of another group of ambitious players using their resources.

For some of the players in Siya's group, many of whom had come from the most prestigious schools in the country, the basic facilities at the WPRI may have felt like a step down from the luxury they had been used to at their private schools, but Siya wasn't about to complain. After all, he didn't have another career to fall back on, or a university degree programme that he could switch to. He had made a commitment to rugby a long time ago and it was working for him. He was well aware of how many young black school stars didn't get to make the leap into professional rugby. Their families simply didn't have the resources to put in the time and focus that was required. This was his chance and he was going to take it.

On arrival at the Institute, the players were allocated a room and someone to share it with, and were given a quick orientation tour of the facility. Many of the boys had been driven to the university by their parents, who milled around until Jacques Hanekom made a short speech, reassuring them that their sons were in good hands and letting them say their goodbyes.

Hanekom is a big, thoughtful man with a quick laugh and a deep understanding of what it takes to bring out the best in a young player. The rugby community first became aware of his coaching prowess when, as a young man, he led Paul Roos Gimnasium to an undefeated season in 1991, and he was one of the first coaches to put together a meaningful and effective programme for young players who were turning professional.

Hanging around in those first few hours, Siya began to get to know some of the players he'd be living and playing with over the next year. Nizaam Carr was a natural loose forward and all-round athlete. He was from Mitchells Plain in Cape Town but he'd grown up in Rondebosch East and completed his schooling at Bishops. He was the only Muslim guy entering the Institute that day. A few doors down from Siya was Frans Malherbe, a young tighthead prop from Paarl Boys' High whom Siya had played against a number of times. Malherbe had captained the first team, and everyone had always presumed that one day he would be Springbok captain.

There was no ignoring the one player in the group who had to bow his head when he walked into his dorm room. Eben Etzebeth was over two metres tall and weighed 120 kilograms. Siya introduced himself and found out that Eben had been a star player at Tygerberg High School, which was not one of the traditional power rugby schools that Grey had travelled to play against.

All around him were incredible young sportsmen, eager to get to work and make a name for themselves. They had all been looking forward to this day for a long time. Siya quickly got a sense of how talented this group of players was going to be and how hard he would have to work to stand out. But he was up for it.

After lunch on that first day, the players began the programme that would consume them for the rest of the year. Ironically, the first order of business was injuries and how to deal with them. 'In our first few years,' says Hanekom, 'nearly 40 per cent of the players who came to the Institute were carrying an injury of some sort. Our first job is to get those injuries to resurface so we can address them quickly.' For the first 72 hours none of the players went near a rugby ball. Instead they were tested extensively on every aspect of their physical performance. Musculoskeletal, endurance, sprints, explosiveness ... each test designed to bring out the best in the players and prepare them for the rigours of life as a professional athlete.

There were 52 players in the programme, which is the perfect number according to Hanekom. 'If you take all the injured players out in a year, there would still be enough for two teams to play each other,' he said.

Hanekom was the first director of the programme. Along with former Springbok coach Nick Mallett, he had chosen a young coach called Steph Nel to write the curriculum and run the programme. Nel had been highly successful at academy level in South Africa before taking up coaching positions in Ireland with Connacht and then Ireland 'A'. That was where he was working when the call came from SA Rugby, the commercial arm of SARU. Nel and his wife had just had a baby, and were looking at making a move back to South Africa, when they found out that the WPRI needed a head coach. He gladly accepted the job.

In Ireland, Nel had worked under Dr Liam Hennessy, the legendary director of fitness at Irish Rugby, who had revolutionised the way Nel thought about coaching. Hennessy's approach to strength and conditioning was markedly different to the South African way of thinking at the time, which was fixated on building big athletes by having them eat lots of pasta and go on long endurance runs. 'Liam was the first guy insisting on data and planning. He understood that the coaching process requires planning, and the process needs to be reviewed and recorded,' says Nel.

The programme Nel devised was gruelling, and as a coach he was as tough as they come, but the boys took it on and began to thrive. The days turned into weeks, friendships deepened, rivalries blossomed, and young professional athletes were built from the ground up.

It was around this time that Siya would have first met Rassie Erasmus, the former Springbok flanker and captain who was then operating as Western Province's senior professional coach. His role was to take an overall view of the strategy, tactics and player recruitment for the entire franchise, so he would have been intimately involved with every annual intake at the WPRI.

With players of the calibre of Eben Etzebeth, Scarra Ntubeni, Nizaam Carr and Frans Malherbe competing for places, the standard at the Institute was high, and there was a palpable air of excitement about this particular group of players. 'They were astonishing,' says Steph Nel. 'Not only their rugby ability, but they were characters. All of them. From the first day I saw Siya, you could sense that this guy has the X factor ... it was just something really special. It was a spark in his eye and that belief that no one is going to stand in my way.'

It wasn't long before people began to believe that they were looking at the core of a future Springbok pack.

* * *

Zwide was never far from Siya's mind. He often wondered what had become of his siblings, Liyema and Liphelo. The last he had heard, they had gone to live with their father after his mother had died. But Siya did not know who that man was nor where the children were living, and he had no idea how to get in touch with them. Also, his life was so busy that he never had the time to start investigating.

During those first few months in Stellenbosch, he did have one chance to go back to Zwide and look for them. But things didn't go to plan, and Siya found himself in trouble as the sun was setting, in a part of town he didn't recognise, with people he didn't know. From out of nowhere, he felt the butt of a nine-millimetre pistol across the back of his head, and he woke up to find all his stuff gone and no one in sight. Steph Nel remembers that 'Scarra brought him back to us the following night, all bruised and in a state of shock. We used to call Scarra "Siya's wife". He was always looking out for him.'

He was fine, but the attack only made Siya worry more about his siblings and the kind of life they were living. But, after a few days, he forced himself to focus on the work and on contributing to the squad however he could.

* * *

There were two categories of players at the Institute: those who had been selected to be part of the programme by the scouts and coaching staff of Western Province, and those who believed they were good enough to be there and were pre-pared to pay and compete for a place in a professional team. The split was about 50:50, but once they got to the WPRI and the programme began, all the players were treated equally, despite the fact that half of the team were being paid a salary for the first time while the other half were paying to be there.

The way the payment system worked was that if they had made Craven Week, then they got a certain amount of money, if they'd also played SA Schools, then they made a little more, and so on. They were graded according to their experience at the top level of schoolboy rugby. But the salary was basic and nobody was there for the money. 'I had two options,' says Hanekom. 'I could give them each a little bit of money, and then provide everything that they needed in terms of food and accommodation and facilities, or I could give them a lot of money and let them make their own plans.' Hanekom and the staff decided on the first option, and it paid off handsomely.

In the first year, they were modestly hoping that five per cent of their players would turn pro. Ten years later, they could look back at the statistics and see that they had far exceeded those humble goals. Forty per cent of the people going through the Stellenbosch programme, both when it started as part of the university and when it morphed into the Stellenbosch Academy of Sport (SAS), have played in the Currie Cup. Twenty per cent of them played Super Rugby and eight per cent became Springboks. In fact, the percentage of Springboks from the programme exceeds the total number of professional players they were aiming for in 2007!

This was not high school any more. Nobody was going to tell the boys not to go out at night, not to have another drink, not to stay out late. Girls could come and visit them in their rooms, but they couldn't stay over – not because of any moral judgement, but just because it would get awkward for their roommates. Many of the players had their own cars and driving licences, and for most this was the first time they had lived far away from home with a bit of money in their pockets.

In a town like Stellenbosch, with its student culture, its

wine and craft beer, great restaurants and bars, and its tolerant attitude towards young people, fun was tough to avoid. There were no classes offered in self-control and discipline, yet these are two of the most vital skills a young rugby player needs to develop. After all, there were plenty of opportunities to indulge in the good life and celebrate your successes, both real and imagined.

The only thing that mattered was the quality of your training. Were you there on time the next morning? Were you able to perform? There were no rules, but there was a three-strike policy for players who crossed the line. The first time that you missed a training session without a valid excuse, you got a warning. The second time, you were sent home to your parents for two weeks. The third time, you were off the programme.

Despite the many temptations, discipline problems were few and far between. The players were motivated to be there and they knew what was required of them. They were under no illusion that they could train all day and party all night – not when they were training from six in the morning to five in the afternoon, six days a week.

A typical week would see the forwards out on the field on Monday morning by 6 am, working on scrums, line-outs and handling. Breakfast was at 7.30, followed by an injury report and squad meeting at 9. They then went back on the field until they broke for lunch at 12.30. There were a few hours for rehab in the early afternoon before the final training session from 4 to 5 pm, when the focus was on the individual player. Supper was at 6 pm, after which the players were free until 6 am the following morning, when the cycle began again.

'Those early-morning sessions are when you find out if a player's still coachable when he's fatigued,' explains

Hanekom. 'Does he still have a nice personality when he's tired and doesn't feel like training?' All these are factors in determining whether or not someone has what it takes to go all the way into the professional ranks.

For everyone at the WPRI, May loomed as the month when their fate would be decided. That was when half of the players would be selected for the Western Province Under-19 squad. Those not chosen faced a far more uncertain future, competing for places in other teams where they hoped their talents would be recognised. This prospect alone was motivation enough to keep them focused on their training.

January to mid-March was the foundation phase, when injuries were discovered and treated and the player's bad habits were deconstructed. After that came the development phase, in which players studied the Western Province approach to the game and learned how to eat properly, look after themselves and manage their money and all that came with being a professional rugby player in a rugby-mad country.

After foundation and development came the phase known as self-awareness, which took place towards the end of May. Everyone dreaded this phase, which was when the players would meet with the coach and learn if they were going through easily, or if their path to the top was going to be a lot harder. 'It leads to an awkward situation where you have a very happy crowd and a very sad crowd all living together,' Hanekom explains. 'The happy crowd is easy to manage after that point, so a lot of focus then goes onto the sad crowd.'

With such a strong intake of players in 2010, the coaches had to look for ways to separate the good from the great. They knew that everyone there could play. They had all been selected for their athleticism and attacking skills, but there was one area of the game where most of the players were slightly under-tested, and that was defence. The reason was obvious. Most of the players came from brilliant rugby schools that easily won most of their games. 'They were recruited for their attacking ability, they were used to getting ball,' says Hanekom. It wasn't often that they had spent an entire game on the back foot defending for their lives. But of course, that's half the game. 'If you can't defend, then you can't play the game.'

The art of defence felt like a lifeline to the players who were paying to be at the Institute. A couple of crunching tackles on one of the big stars was a great way to get noticed, and if you could show the coach your courage and stamina when the game was not going your way, then you were in with a shot. 'You get the fancy guys thinking they're God's gift to rugby, and then you have the pay-to-play guys who say to themselves, "I only have to hunt you down and then I'm in the team," so it's very motivating to both sides,' says Hanekom. Playing defence was a great equaliser for all the boys coming through the programme, and it fed into an atmosphere of healthy competition. With that competitive edge came transparency as well. Everyone could see who was up and who was down, and when a star player was replaced in the final squad, everyone understood the reasons for it. 'I used to hate tackling at school,' Siya admitted in 2014. 'I came to Western Province and I had to tackle every single day. And I started loving it, especially when I hit someone hard.'

For Siya, one of the biggest adjustments he had to make in those first six months out of school was the lack of game time. The staff who planned the programme firmly believed that the players had played enough competitive rugby matches at schoolboy level. This was a time for coaching. Hanekom is philosophical about his approach. 'As soon as the focus is games,' he says, 'you fall into a rhythm of preparation and recovery, week in and week out, and there's no room for coaching.'

Instead of game time, the players' new focus becomes the ability to reach the specific workload they must be able to handle as a professional rugby player, week in and week out, which they call 'chasing the load'. Getting to that load, staying there and being able to function is the goal of the first six months at the Institute. The way it works is that players must rate everything they do on a scale from one to ten, from the quality of sleep to the intensity of a workout, and find a way to make their load numbers week in and week out.

The players get into a routine of working six-day weeks for two and a half weeks and then taking four days off to complete a three-week cycle. Then it begins again, and as the weeks turn into months, it starts to become clear who has got the willpower and the drive to stick it out at this level.

It's vital for the health of the whole programme that the 26 players not selected for the Western Province Under-19 team stay motivated and committed to the programme. Their journey is far from over, and if they can learn from their mistakes and redouble their efforts, then many of them will go on to play the game at the highest level. Making the cut in May is a reality check that will inform the rest of the year for them.

There are many examples of players who missed the cut but carried on to have stellar careers. Andries Coetzee is one example. He wasn't selected, but Jacques Hanekom told him to just hang in there and keep playing. A few months later, he was chosen to be part of the Bulls Under-21 team, then he played for Tukkies and was selected for the Lions to play in the Currie Cup and then Super Rugby. In 2017, Coetzee made his Springbok debut, a long journey from that agonising meeting in mid-May 2009 when he was told he hadn't made the cut.

9
■

Turning Pro

Being selected to join the Western Province Under-19 squad wasn't the only awesome thing that happened in 2010. Siya was also thrilled to be selected for the Under-20 Springbok squad, known as the 'Baby Boks'. It was a great honour and a chance to get some real international experience under his belt.

The Baby Boks were due to travel to Argentina for a three-game tour a few weeks before the IRB Junior World Championship tournament, which was set to kick off in June in Buenos Aires. The team gathered for a series of training camps in Cape Town and Johannesburg, and Siya got a chance to train with players such as CJ Stander, Patrick Lambie, Elton Jantjies and S'bura Sithole who were rising through the ranks of South African rugby. He knew many of them from Craven Week, and he had followed their careers in the press, but since his arrival in Stellenbosch there had been almost no travelling and no big matches.

The Junior World Championship was a relatively new tournament that had been established in 2008 to replace the Under-19 and Under-21 designations. The first tournament of the new format had taken place in Wales, the second in Japan – both won by New Zealand, who had beaten England resoundingly in both finals. South Africa had come third twice in a row. In 2010, they arrived in Argentina hungry to make it all the way to the final.

The whole tournament lasted just two weeks, so there was a lot of pressure on the players to achieve peak fitness, to recover quickly between games, and to pace themselves for the 14-day period. Typically, there was a game on the Saturday, then a few days to travel and recover before a game on Wednesday, then on to the next game the following Saturday. It was intense and exhausting but also thrilling, and a wonderful lesson on what it was like to travel and play internationally.

The players loved the laid-back vibe of Argentina, with its neoclassical architecture, passion for sports and love of good food and wine. It felt like home to a lot of them.

The opening match of Pool C was a fairly easy 40–14 victory over Tonga – just the right way to start a tournament. In the second game of the group, everything went right for the Baby Boks and they recorded a staggering 73–0 victory over Scotland. Siya was ecstatic: he scored a try in the ninth minute of the game and then broke through the line for another try only three minutes later. These represented his first official points for his country, and he couldn't have been happier. Flyhalf Patrick Lambie had an outstanding game, scoring 29 points for the team and combining beautifully with the pack and the backline.

The Under-20s were proud that they had not lost a single game during the pool phase at the Junior World Championship since it began, but that record was put to the test in their final Group C pool match in 2010 when they came up against

Australia in the city of Santa Fe. Lambie opened the scoring with a penalty in the first minute of the game, and Wandile Mjekevu followed up with a try in the eighth minute, but Australia kept their composure, didn't panic, and came back to score ten points in three minutes to stay in the game. It was a see-saw battle: every time one team pulled into the lead, the other team found a way to claw their way back into it. It was only a try for Australia from Ed Quirk in the 64th minute and a final penalty from Matthew To'omua in the 76th that separated the two teams at the end.

The South Africans were disappointed to have lost but relieved that they still qualified for the semi-finals by virtue of having the best record of all the second-place teams, thanks to that massive victory over Scotland.

The semi-final against the defending champions, New Zealand, was never going to be easy. After all, the Kiwis had won all their pool games, scoring over 40 points per game to end with a massive 164 points in total.

The team travelled 300 kilometres northwest of Buenos Aires to the city of Rosario for the semi-finals. From the first moments of the game, the All Blacks came out firing and were able to release Julian Savea down the wing for a try in the first five minutes. The Baby Boks defended bravely but the scoreboard kept ticking up on the Kiwi side, and it was only in injury time at the end of the first half that the Boks managed to get scrumhalf Branco du Preez over the line and convert the try for seven points.

But it wasn't enough. By the end of the game they had lost badly, 36–7, and their dreams of making it into the finals for the first time lay in tatters.

Still, after the defeat there was no deviation from the

tournament schedule. The team had to contest a third-place playoff against England, who had beaten them in the semi-finals the previous year. It was a chance to take some revenge and the Springboks seized it, scoring four tries and a penalty to end up five points ahead at 27–22. Siya played at number 6 in that game and put in a huge effort, with some great support play and stalwart defence, before being replaced by Tera Mtembu in the 68th minute.

For the third year in a row, the Baby Boks had finished third in the tournament, satisfied with how they had played but determined to make the finals next time.

* * *

Returning to Stellenbosch, Siya had a few weeks to rest and recover before the second part of the WPRI programme began. The players selected for the Western Province Under-19 squad gathered again on 28 June and started working on their campaign. This was the first time that Siya would be part of a provincial squad touring South Africa week in and week out. It was something that all the players had been dreaming about since they became friends and team-mates.

There is nothing like being on the road together to bond a group of players into a team. The planes and buses, hotels and stadiums – it was all going to be a big adventure and a chance to see the country. The team trained with a new intensity before setting off to play in places like Bloemfontein, Potchefstroom and Welkom and to get used to the rhythm of the life of a touring professional.

The Under-19 Western Province team performed well all season and made it all the way into the Absa Under-19 interprovincial finals, where they came up against the Vodacom Blue Bulls at the Absa Stadium in Durban. The energy on the pitch was crackling and both teams came out hard. The Bulls piled on the pressure but Province held on strongly and did well to give away only six points in the first 20 minutes. Then Bulls hooker Jacques Moolman was sent off for a high tackle and Province ratcheted up the pressure, releasing scrumhalf Ricky Schroeder over the line for a first try and Scarra for the second, moments before half-time, to go into the break leading 20 points to 6.

The Bulls came out after the break with all guns blazing and raced over for two quick tries. Both were converted and suddenly the scores were level again. For a while it looked like all the hard work that the team had done at the Institute wouldn't be enough to crown them Under-19 champions, but flyhalf William van Wyk kept his cool, slotting his second drop goal of the day to give Province a three-point cushion.

In the final few minutes of the second half, the Blue Bulls won the chance to add three more easy points, but instead they elected to kick for the corner and go for the try. But the kick went wrong and rolled over the dead-ball line and the advantage was squandered. Siya could see the opposition drop their shoulders slightly and realised they were now firmly on the back foot.

Province kept their composure and added three more points just before the final whistle to win the game 26 to 20. This was Siya's first trophy win for his new club and it felt fantastic.

It was a spectacular way to complete a strong transitional year for Siya, a year in which he had taken all the potential he had shown at schoolboy level and transformed himself into one of the most highly rated juniors in the country.

He left the WPRI having made friendships that would last a lifetime, and he couldn't wait to be playing regularly with his team-mates in front of the Newlands fans in the upcoming Vodacom Cup. If things went according to plan, there might even be a debut start for the Stormers.

10

—

Moving On Up

Once the training programme at the Institute came to an end, Siya and Scarra moved in with Steph Nel's family for a few months. They had become close to Nel's children, and repaid the family with hours of babysitting duties, but at the beginning of 2011 they decided to find communal digs in Cape Town. They moved in with Eben Etzebeth and Siya's old friend Nick Holton, who was studying at UCT and playing success-fully for Ikeys.

Training moved from Stellenbosch University to the Western Province Rugby High Performance Centre (HPC) in Bellville, which had opened its doors in 2008. The HPC is a state-of-the-art facility boasting two full-size training fields, a gymnasium and two doctors in attendance at all times, as well as audiovisual capabilities and sports science, catering and recreational facilities.

Bringing together everything that the players and the coaching staff needed in one place had made an enormous impact on Western Province rugby. 'Western Province now have a facility that allows us to carry out [immediately] functions that in the past may have taken four days to carry out,' said the director of rugby, Rassie Erasmus, to the press. Erasmus was not only director of rugby but also coach of the Stormers, and it was beneficial for him to be able to monitor how players from all the teams were performing on a daily basis.

The very best facilities at the HPC were reserved for the senior players, and this helped to incentivise the Under-21s to see if they could find a way into the senior ranks.

The training schedule at the HPC was similar to the WPRI, and to what Siya had been used to at Grey. Mondays and Tuesdays were when the heavy training was done. Wednesday was a rest day, although the players often had media and promotional duties to fulfil. Thursday was a half-day, and on Fridays there was either a Captain's Run, in which the captain of the team took over the coaching role, or there was travel to an away game.

The first order of business for Western Province in 2011 was the Vodacom Cup, which takes place between February and May each year. The coach was John Dobson, a Capetonian born and raised who had done well coaching the UCT Ikeys in the Varsity Cup. He had been scheduled to take up a coaching job in Italy in 2010 but the deal had fallen through. Italian rugby's loss was Western Province rugby's gain. Dobson joined Province and immediately made an impact, coaching the Under-21s all the way to a win in the 2010 Under-21 Provincial Championship and earning himself a promotion to Vodacom Cup coach.

The Vodacom Cup is played at a high level, but without all the frills and glamour of the Currie Cup or Super Rugby. But it's a vital step on the journey for young players. Dobson understood the role of the competition well. 'The reality is that it's hard to go from club or Varsity Cup rugby to Vodacom Super Rugby,' he said. 'We provide a bridging role. For a union like ours, it allows us to provide opportunities to young, promising and club players, as well as doing our core function, which is to add to the depth of the DHL Stormers.'

Siya played his first game for Western Province on 26 February 2011 against the Golden Lions. When he pulled on the blue-and-white stripes in front of 7 000 fans at Newlands that day, it was the culmination of a long journey from the streets of Zwide to first-class rugby. That first game was a gruelling affair, but it was also the start of a whole new part of his career that would hopefully take him all the way to the Rugby World Cup. It was a tough match and a timely reminder that standards were getting higher and higher every time he made the leap into a new division.

Jannie Boshoff scored first for the Lions down the wing, before centre Johann Sadie burst through the Lions backline to equalise for Western Province in the 36th minute. The game remained all square until the 72nd minute when the Lions scored again with a try from hooker Edgar Marutlulle. But Province had brought their kicking boots to Newlands that day and they regularly added three points with kicks from Kurt Coleman and Sam Lane, as well as a drop kick from the American-born Marcel Brache. It was great to be back on the same team as Kurt Coleman, who had graduated from Grey High School and then the WPRI a year ahead of Siya. It must have almost felt like school again to see the ball leaving Kurt's boot and sailing through the posts in the 80th minute of the game to bring the scores level at 18–18.

The following weekend, Siya scored his first try for Province when they demolished the Falcons by 86 points to 14 in

Kempton Park, and again the week after that when they put 56 points over against the Welwitschias, the Namibian national side. The players were gelling nicely. Lionel Cronjé was on a strong run of form, and players like JJ Engelbrecht and Louis Schreuder were scoring easily and running a highly effective backline.

Western Province finished the Southern Section of the competition undefeated, with only that first draw against the Lions as a blemish on a perfect record. John Dobson and the rest of the coaching staff were delighted, and the team's success augured well for the future. Not only were they the youngest and most diverse team in the competition, but they also had the most amateurs coming through to play for the professional side. It was a testament to all the work that had gone into the union, at every level, from the WPRI all the way to the Stormers.

The quarter-final of the Vodacom Cup saw Western Province come up against a passionate Sharks side at Newlands. Both teams were feeling the pressure, though, and the game never really got going. The Sharks scored first when winger Mark Richards found some space and belted towards the corner, beating four Province tacklers in the process. Four minutes later, Province won a turnover on their ten-metre line and spun the ball down the line to JJ Engelbrecht, who sprinted past the cover defence, set his sights on the try line, and was simply unstoppable on his way to five more points.

The Sharks went into the break leading by 15 points to 8, but some solid kicking from flyhalf Demetri Catrakilis kept Western Province in the hunt. With only three minutes to go, Province were down by 21 to 19. A try from Danie Poolman brought them back to within two points, but the angle on the conversion was too acute for Catrakilis and the game finished with Province two points behind. It was a sad end to what had been such a stellar season for the young team.

The only disappointment that Siya felt was that senior coach Rassie Erasmus would be leaving Western Province and joining the Springbok setup ahead of the upcoming 2011 Rugby World Cup campaign. Siya had enjoyed working with the senior professional coach and would miss Erasmus's input into his on-field development.

* * *

There wasn't much time to dwell on what could have been in the Vodacom Cup. Siya had a few weeks to relax before he set his mind to the next challenge: the 2011 Junior Rugby Championship in Italy, starting on 10 June, just a few days before his 20th birthday. The Baby Boks had been drawn in Pool C with England, Scotland and Ireland – all good teams that demanded respect and good planning. But the South Africans felt confident as they gathered in early June for a training camp ahead of the campaign. There were some fantastic young players in that team, led by captain Arno Botha, and Siya couldn't wait to play on the same side as guys like Courtnall Skosan, Ruan Venter and the young Blue Bulls hooker Bongi Mbonambi, as well as regular team-mates like Eben Etzebeth.

England was the opponent that worried them the most. The Springboks cruised past Scotland 33–0 in their first game, played in the northern city of Padua, and then past Ireland four days later by 42 points to 26, thanks to tries from Eben Etzebeth, Wandile Mjekevu, Arno Botha and inside centre Jacobus Venter, who scored twice. England also won their first two games, and everything was set up for the big final clash of Pool C.

Meanwhile, the Western Province players were following the results from the Super Rugby tournament closely. The Stormers had done fantastically well, winning the South African conference with 63 points, ahead of the Sharks on 57 and the Bulls on 54, which meant they were in second position overall behind the Queensland Reds and scheduled to face the Crusaders in the semi-final at Newlands on 2 July.

But the success had come at a cost. Both eighth man Duane Vermeulen and flanker Pieter Louw had picked up season-ending knee injuries. Suddenly Siya was next in line to make his debut for the Stormers, so he wasn't all that surprised when he got a call-up for his senior team while he was still in Italy. This was exactly the kind of opportunity he needed to get a foot in the door at the Stormers. But the first order of business was the final group match against England, scheduled for Padua's Stadio Plebiscito on 18 June.

England started well and won a penalty in the first two minutes, which was converted by flyhalf George Ford. After the restart, they took back possession and spread the ball down the line towards fullback Elliot Daly, who crashed over for another five points. The Boks were unable to make any headway and were lucky to stay in the game when England missed out on another five points due to a missed conversion and a missed penalty.

Finally, the South Africans found their rhythm when Nizaam Carr crossed the line in the 25th minute to get the score back up to a respectable 8–5. Johan Goosen missed the conversion but slotted two penalties before the first half ended with the scores tied at 11–11.

The second half got off to a bad start for the Boks. Alex Gray broke through the line for a try, but George Ford was not having a good day with the boot and he missed another conversion. Once again, Goosen kept his team in the match with another penalty. Siya had worked hard to tie in with the backline, and to exert maximum pressure at the breakdowns, but by the 52nd minute he was flagging badly, so he was replaced by Cornell du Preez. The South Africans played their hearts out for the rest of the game but they were never able to pull level, and when the England winger Christian Wade darted in for a try in the 70th minute and made the score 24–17, the team began to feel the game slipping away. One more penalty from Goosen wasn't enough and the game ended 20–26.

The South Africans were deeply disappointed. This was the first time in the Junior Championship that they had lost during the group phase, and the atmosphere in the camp was gloomy as Siya said his goodbyes and headed back to Cape Town to join the Stormers.

At home, rugby fever had taken hold of Cape Town in the run-up to the crucial Super 15 semi-final against the Crusaders. Tickets to the game were sold out weeks in advance, and the newspapers speculated feverishly about which team had the advantage and what it would take to win. Both Stormers coach Allister Coetzee and Todd Blackadder of the Crusaders heaped praise on the opposition and tried to play down the occasion. It wasn't hard to find reasons to praise the Crusaders. With superstars like Dan Carter and Richie McCaw in the team, they were a formidable force. They had beaten the Stormers in eight of the last ten games they had played, and even home advantage was nullified because they had such a passionate fanbase in Cape Town.

Joining the Stormers team back at the HPC, Siya worked hard to learn the game plan and slot into the squad. For so long, he had dreamed about working in the senior section of the HPC, and of playing in the same team as legends like Schalk Burger and Bryan Habana. He was determined to be an asset on the field.

The Stormers took a much-needed break on the weekend before the big match against the Crusaders. This was exactly what Siya needed after the heavy training schedule of the last few months. He made a plan to go out on the town with Scarra and take their minds off rugby completely. But something happened that night that changed the course of the season for Siya. The two players were mugged by a knife-wielding assailant somewhere off Long Street in Cape Town. Details of the incident are sketchy, but there was some kind of a scuffle and Siya sustained a concussion, as well as a shoulder and wrist injury. He was badly shaken. 'He is in no physical or mental condition to play this weekend,' Stormers coach Allister Coetzee said afterwards.

Siya was devastated, and the Stormers were thrown back into chaos. This was the third loose forward they had lost before this crucial game. The management team put their heads together on Saturday and came up with a plan. They would ask UK club Saracens if they could release their hooker, Schalk Brits, to come and play one game as a flank for the Stormers. Coetzee remembers that the team 'cast the net wide, but decided to call in Schalk Brits. He has been part of our system in the past, he understands the Stormers and will bring that impact we need from the bench at a crucial time in the second half.'

Brits was granted permission to play and flew out from

London the following evening to join the Stormers. It was a low point for Siya, who was angry that his big chance had slipped away right before the end of the season. This was one of those moments he'd been waiting for his whole life. To get so close, then to see it slip through his fingers, was devastating, especially as the missed opportunity had nothing to do with his performance on the field. Now he would have to wait another whole year before he would make his Stormers debut. His frustration only deepened on the day of the game when the Crusaders ran rings around the Cape Town team and ended up beating them by 29 points to 10. Siya felt like he'd let the side down.

11

Living the Dream

The next milestone for Siya was to make the move up to Currie Cup level. Even though he had competed regularly for Western Province during the Vodacom Cup, it still felt like a significant move when he lined up to play against Griquas in the Currie Cup at Newlands on 16 July.

The first try of the match came from Griquas winger Rocco Jansen. He gathered the ball on the halfway line, and ran hard until he was facing a one-on-one situation. He chipped the ball through, darted around the defender, and gathered to dive over the line to score.

Ten minutes later, Province won a scrum in the centre of the field. The ball was fed down the line but a great tackle stopped the movement. Siya hung back as the WP scrum-half gathered the ball and darted towards the openside, then did a quick reverse pass as Siya burst through the line and into space. The switch and the change of direction bamboozled the Griquas defence, and all that was left was for Siya to dive under the posts and record his first Currie Cup points. Scoring a try was a great feeling and his confidence surged. Later in the game, he nearly got a second try, and it was only a game-saving tackle from two Griquas players that kept him a few centimetres short of the line.

The game ended on 26 points apiece. This was the only draw of that 2011 season for Province, who won eight of their games and lost five, finishing in fourth position on the log and qualifying for the playoffs.

They came up against the Golden Lions in the semi-finals in Johannesburg on 22 October but were put to the sword by Elton Jantjies, the young flyhalf from the University of Johannesburg who was making such a name for himself in the professional game. Jantjies scored five out of five penalties and a conversion to take the game away from Western Province.

It was another bitter loss for Siya. Province had lost in the semi-finals of the Vodacom Cup, he had missed out on a semi-final slot with the Stormers in the Super 15, and now he had been denied another chance to earn a trophy in the Currie Cup. On the upside, this was a young, dynamic team and they were improving with every game.

* * *

In September 2011, all eyes turned to the Rugby World Cup in New Zealand. As defending champions, South Africa should have been the favourite to win the competition for a third time, but they hadn't had a particularly good year, winning only four of their last eight encounters. But they still had 18 members of the 2007 cup-winning team, including captain John Smit, the awe-inspiring combination of Victor Matfield and Bakkies Botha in the pack, alongside younger talent like WP's Juan de Jongh as well as Pat Lambie and Odwa Ndungane from the Sharks. On paper, the team was as good as any South Africa had ever produced, and the country was looking forward to a robust campaign.

The Springboks had been lucky when the groups were selected. They were drawn in Group D, with Wales, Fiji, Samoa and Namibia, and it was only the Welsh who provided any stiff opposition. In their first game, the Springboks won narrowly by 17 to 16 against the Welsh, but they were able to score nearly 100 points against Namibia and almost 50 against Samoa. By the time they lined up in the quarter-final against Australia in Wellington on 9 October, there was a sense that the Boks hadn't really been tested for nearly a month.

Meanwhile, in the Currie Cup, Western Province had just been resoundingly beaten by the Golden Lions in Johannesburg the day before. The team travelled home and went their separate ways. Siya returned to the house he was sharing with a few of his team-mates just in time to watch the World Cup quarter-finals. As the game started, the Springboks dominated in the first scrum and signalled that this pack meant business. All the early backline pressure came from Jean de Villiers and Bryan Habana but they were unable to make it count on the scoreboard. Australia fought back hard and in their first attacking move they were able to score a try and put five points on the board, when the Australian captain James Horwill barged over the line after the Springbok ball was turned over only five metres from the line.

Australia were energised by that try. A few minutes later, Kurtley Beale gathered the ball and ran hard at the Boks, making 35 metres before offloading to Stephen Moore, who was tackled heavily by Schalk Burger, who was himself forced to leave the field with an injury moments later. Then Jannie du Plessis was penalised for handling on the ground and Australia converted to make the score 8–0.

Schalk Burger came back on the field and threw himself back into attack, but it was only in the 38th minute of the first half that David Pocock conceded a penalty and Morné Steyn converted it to get South Africa on the scoreboard. Just before half-time, Steyn missed another penalty that would have put the Springboks right back into the game.

In the second half, South Africa threw everything they had at the Australians, but the Wallabies' defence held firm. Then, with 24 minutes of the game left, Steyn slotted another penalty kick and the score went to 8–6 in favour of Australia. The South Africans kept the pressure up, won the ball back straight off a line-out, and worked it back down to Morné Steyn, who positioned himself beautifully and slotted a drop kick through the posts in the 60th minute. South Africa inched ahead by a single point.

But, despite all the pressure, Australia kept the Boks out and then forced another penalty in the 70th minute. Unfazed by the Bok attack, the Australians retook the lead at 11–9. Watching from the comfort of his home, Siya could see the frustration building among his countrymen as they struggled to get good-quality balls in the last ten minutes. David Pocock was a titan for Australia, and it sometimes felt like he was single-handedly keeping his team in the game. The clock ticked down and then suddenly it was all over. South Africa, the defending champions, were out of the World Cup. It was a bitter pill for the country to swallow.

After the game, accusations were thrown at the referee and there was a lot of discussion about what could have been if just a few decisions had gone their way, but that was all just talk. The Springboks would be giving up the crown of world champions.

After the World Cup was over, the Western Province Rugby Union had been expecting Rassie Erasmus to return as senior professional coach, and they were a little dismayed when he announced that he would not be returning and that he was investigating some overseas job offers instead.

* * *

Turning up for practice in Bellville the next week, Siya tried to throw off the gloom that he felt, but it was no use. The whole country was in a sporting depression over what might have been. At the same time as the rest of the World Cup was unfolding, the Currie Cup was reaching its climax. Province recorded an easy home win against the Pumas, then travelled up to Johannesburg for a semi-final against the Lions. It was an uphill battle from the first whistle, and Elton Jantjies was in devastating form with the boot, successfully launching the ball between the posts for five penalties, one conversion and a drop kick. Province couldn't come back, despite their best efforts and at the end of the game the scoreboard showed them down 20–29.

Meanwhile, the World Cup came to a conclusion when New Zealand took on France and beat them in a closely fought final, marking the third time that a host country had won the tournament. It was also New Zealand's fourth World Cup win.

It had been another disappointing end of season for Siya. His first year as a professional had been incredible, and he could be justifiably proud of the way he had handled the transition to professional rank. But there was simply no substitute for winning titles, and again and again he'd seen his team come close but not quite take it all the way. He was determined to change that in 2012, and to convert all these great opportunities into trophies.

12

A Life-Changing Year

Siya approached the beginning of the 2012 season in a positive frame of mind. His off-season training had gone well and he had been named as a member of the Stormers squad for the Super 15 rugby season. The only downside was that he had once again gone back to Zwide and tried to find his siblings, but without any luck. It had been over three years since his mother's death and he still had no idea what had happened to Liyema and Liphelo. But he knew he was finally in a position to be able to help the two kids, and nothing was going to get in his way.

On the field, he was settling into his position as openside flanker, where his pace and exceptional ball-handling skills could be best utilised. Away from the game, he was really enjoying life in Cape Town. He had a great group of friends, from both inside and outside rugby, and there were many benefits to being part of a beloved rugby franchise in a city such as Cape Town. Even though the players were kept busy for most of the week, there was ample time to enjoy the many perks of living in Cape Town.

But Siya kept his feet on the ground. Just like in high

school, when he arranged for buses to go and pick people up in Zwide to come and watch a match, Siya was still passionate about spreading the word and getting people into the stadium who normally would not (or could not) turn out for matches. Kendra Houghton remembers how Siya used to go out into the streets 'with 20 burgers and 20 tickets' and give them away to people before a match. 'No one knew about it, it was just something genuine that he wanted to do.'

The first game of the new season was scheduled for 25 February at Newlands. The Stormers were up against the Hurricanes, the team from Wellington, New Zealand. The Hurricanes had finished a disappointing ninth in the previous season's competition, but they had some great players, such as Beauden Barrett, Conrad Smith and Dane Coles, and they were determined to start their season off with a victory that would set the course.

Naturally, the Stormers had the same goal in mind.

Siya was on the bench, alongside Scarra and Frans Malherbe, as the season began. The Stormers pack was formidable: Steven Kitshoff, Tiaan Liebenberg and Brok Harris were in the front row; Eben Etzebeth, making his first start for the Stormers, and the experienced Andries Bekker were paired up as locks; and Duane Vermeulen and Schalk Burger were in the flank positions, with Nick Koster as eighth man. They were all great ball players, and many were saying this was one of the strongest packs that the Stormers had ever fielded. Siya knew that he was in good company, and that if he could break into this team, they would lift his game to new heights.

The Stormers started well, with Gio Aplon finding space early on for a try in the third minute and an easy conversion by Joe Pietersen. The Stormers were very physical on defence and they challenged aggressively for everything. Schalk Burger in particular was an absolute warrior on defence, but a crunching tackle from Tristan Moran saw Burger falling to the ground in pain, clutching his knee, and hobbling off. Moran's 'reward' for the foul was ten minutes in the sin bin, but on the upside, this was Siya's chance to make his Super Rugby debut.

A few moments later and the Stormers won a line-out on the Hurricanes' 22-metre line. Liebenberg found Andries Bekker high in the air, and he held on to the ball as a maul formed around him. Moments later, the ball found its way back to Siya, who grasped it in his right hand and stayed locked into the maul as the Stormers built some momentum and surged forwards. All Siya had to do was hold on and fall over the line, and that's exactly what he did – the first try for the Stormers in his first few minutes on the field. The look on his face showed that he could hardly believe it was real until captain Jean de Villiers came running over and lifted Siya up off his feet in a massive hug.

'What a debut moment for Siya Kolisi!' cheered the TV commentator as shots of Scarra celebrating on the try line filled the screen. After the conversion, the Stormers were up 14–6 and ready to run rampant. But the Hurricanes flyhalf Beauden Barrett had other ideas and he kept his team in the game with a great offload to Timmy Bateman, who went over just before the half-time whistle. Bateman followed this up with a brilliant solo effort after half-time, when he intercepted a pass out to the wing and ran down half the field, chased by Gio Aplon, to score.

Barrett kicked 16 points during that game, but Joe Pietersen matched his performance and ended up with 21 points in his column to help the Stormers finish ahead 39 points to 26. A win

115

in the first game of the season, and the Stormers found themselves in fourth position.

The elation in the Stormers' change room was tempered by the news that Schalk Burger's knee injury was worse than anticipated and that he would be ruled out for at least a few months. It was a devastating blow for Burger and the team, but a golden opportunity for Siya to show his team-mates and the fans what he could do.

This was the start of the most intense season of rugby that Siya had ever experienced. Super 15 Rugby was at a whole new level for him. He would have to contend with the long travel days, jet lag, new people and places and the whole experience of playing in arguably the world's premier rugby competition. All in all, he played in 16 of the 18 games in the regular season, which added up to more than a thousand minutes on the field playing top-quality international rugby in a team that was firing on all cylinders. The Stormers never dropped below fourth position overall that whole season. They were in first or second place for the last six weeks of the competition and ended up top overall with 66 points, two ahead of the Chiefs on 64 and the Reds on 58.

Qualifying in first place earned the Stormers a rest week before the big semi-final clash on 28 July against old rivals the Sharks in front of a home crowd. Siya was fully expecting that he would erase the painful memories of the many times he had come close to a final before falling at the last hurdle.

* * *

Newlands was packed to the rafters early that Saturday afternoon, with a confident home crowd expecting their team to go all the way. The distinctive smell of the hops from the South African Breweries factory filled the air, and contributed to the party atmosphere as the fans streamed down Main Road, over the Liesbeek River and past all the vendors selling Stormers gear around the stadium.

The teams were evenly matched during the first half of the game, with only a drop kick from the superb French midfielder Frédéric Michalak separating them. But then a hoisted up-and-under from Riaan Viljoen was chased down by JP Pietersen and Louis Ludik, who overpowered the Stormers defence. Ludik caught the ball as he landed, spun out of a tackle, darted inside past two defenders, skipping over a desperate ankle tap, and then dived gratefully over the line. It was a sensational moment of individual flair and the Sharks fans in the stadium went berserk.

Halfway through the second half, the Sharks were leading 16–9. They whipped the ball out of the scrum down to winger JP Pietersen, who sliced through the Stormers backline for a second try, followed by a conversion, which saw them going 4 points clear.

A few minutes later, the Stormers' Jean de Villiers and Gio Aplon combined easily for a try down the wing that gave the Stormers a fragile sense of hope, but it was too little, too late, and the game ended 19–26. There was bitter disappointment all around the Cape. Once again, Siya felt the taste of defeat before he had accomplished his goals. Once again, the season was ending on a sour note. They had beaten the Sharks at home in Round Two of the competition, but had lost in Round 14. It could have gone either way, but that moment of magic from Ludik had ultimately been the difference between the teams on the day.

* * *

That was the end of Siya's first season of Super Rugby. There's always something special about your first season – before your opponents and all the commentators know your style, before they have examined and dissected your every move. Siya proved himself over and over again as a team player, as a suitable replacement for Schalk, and as a warrior who was unafraid of the fight. Despite his imposing physique, Siya was not a flashy player who always made the headlines. But his support play, his positional sense, his fierce defending and his speed did not go unnoticed by his team-mates.

In his autobiography, *For the Record*, former Springbok captain Gary Teichmann wrote that 'the second season is the hardest because your opponents have figured you out'. Siya had cemented his place in the team and his opponents had taken note. Now the other teams would be coming for him. Teichmann also spoke about how 'surging runs and dramatic tackles are the things that get noticed', but added that your team-mates recognise it when you're 'doing the hard gains at the bottom of the ruck'. Siya had proven over and over that he was in it purely for the team and not his own status.

His maturity was on display for everyone to see.

This was also true off the field in 2012, when the fun and excitement of being young and single in Cape Town started to wear off. At some point in the year, Siya was invited to a dinner in Stellenbosch and there he met the woman who would become his wife and life partner just a few years later.

Rachel Smith was born in June 1990, a year before Siya. She went to school in Grahamstown before moving with her family to Cape Town after she matriculated. She made a name for herself as an event manager and marketing executive, and was working in marketing for Audi when she met Siya. In an interview with Parent24.com, she remembers how 'Siya and I met at a dinner with mutual friends in Stellenbosch. I didn't think he was anything special that night, actually I thought he was quite rude because he didn't greet us when we arrived. We became very good friends a few months later, and during that time I realised I needed him in my life, somewhere – as a friend, partner, whatever – just somewhere he needed to be there.'

It soon became clear to Siya that there was something very special about Rachel – that she was the one. He began to cut down on the partying and socialising. She was also serious about fitness and training, and helped get him in better shape than he had ever been in before. Siya confessed to *City Press* that he struggled to let Rachel know how he was feeling about her: 'I knew I liked her and had to tell her. It was scary. I asked her to lunch and that's when I told her. She played hard to get in the beginning, but eventually admitted it as well. The rest is history.'

Kendra Houghton remembers how quickly Rachel was able to ground Siya. 'When Rachel came along, she was solid like a rock,' says Kendra. It wasn't too long before Siya began going to church with her, living a clean lifestyle, and the couple started to incorporate fitness and spirituality into their relationship.

* * *

In late May, Siya got the news that he had been waiting his whole life to hear. The Springbok selectors named their squad for the inaugural Castle Rugby Championship, and Siya was selected as part of the 'young guns' squad who would train with the Springboks ahead of their games against England in June. He was over the moon, even though he wouldn't actually be making his Springbok debut. But to be included with some of the best young players of his generation, including prop Pat Cilliers, flyhalf Elton Jantjies, outside centre (and fellow Grey Old Boy) JJ Engelbrecht and scrumhalf Jano Vermaak, was a great vote of confidence.

'Siya [Kolisi] is a very versatile player,' said Springbok coach Heyneke Meyer at the announcement of the squad. 'I see him mostly as an openside flank, but he gives you the options that he can play number 8 and blindside.'

So it was that Siya found himself training with the Springbok squad on 16 June 2012, his 21st birthday. If he had been less busy that day, he might have thought back to his childhood and wondered if there was anywhere on earth he would rather spend his birthday than with the Springboks.

Towards the end of the day, the Springbok management surprised him with a giant cake to celebrate his birthday. Siya was delighted and casually remarked to the squad that it was the first birthday cake he had ever received. It was a sobering reminder to everyone gathered there that day of just how far he had come.

Siya was delighted to see his old comrade Eben Etzebeth included in the squad for the three games against England. Eben's rise to the top of the game had been nothing short of meteoric. Siya was thrilled for him and knew how much he deserved it. He was hopeful that his own international debut was not too far away. During that series, the Springboks won two and drew the final game. Siya rejoined Western Province believing that all he had to do was be patient and put in the work, and the results would come.

Following the Springbok training camp in June, the Springbok selectors announced their final squad selection for the upcoming Castle Rugby Championship in early August This was the new name for the Tri-Nations tournament, which henceforth would include Argentina. Siya waited nervously to hear if he would be part of that squad and was overjoyed when he heard his name come up, along with four other uncapped players. It was a dream come true, and he couldn't wait for the squad to gather the following day to begin preparations for the series.

But before he could focus too narrowly on Springbok duty, there were the first few games of the Currie Cup to take care of.

* * *

In the first round of the Currie Cup, Western Province were drawn in a home clash against the Sharks, which they narrowly lost by 25 points to 23. But they recovered well in Round Two to beat Griquas fairly convincingly in Kimberley, before travelling up to Johannesburg for the third match of the series against the Golden Lions.

Coach Allister Coetzee was frustrated, as injury concerns had been mounting for weeks. He was without the services of Nick Koster, Nizaam Carr, Schalk Burger and Rynhardt Elstadt, and as a result hooker Deon Fourie had been filling in at flank. With all these injuries to deal with, Siya was keenly aware of how important he was to the squad, and he was determined to step up for the team.

Siya hadn't been chosen for the first games of the Springbok tour against Argentina, so he was playing for Province on the day that the Springboks were playing Round Two of the Rugby Championship against Argentina. He was determined to show he should have been in the Springbok squad that day, but the rugby gods had other plans. During the game against the Golden Lions, Siya felt a sharp crack in his left hand and knew immediately that he was in trouble. An X-ray after the game revealed that he had broken his left thumb and that it would require surgery to put right. This meant he would miss out on the rest of the Currie Cup season and his dreams of making his Springbok debut in that year's Rugby Championship.

It was a devastating way for the season to end.

The only consolation was the show of support from Heyneke Meyer, who told the press: 'It's obviously very disappointing news. Siya's a great player with a lot of character and he was always part of the plans going forward. I wanted to blend him in and get him in slowly and give him the necessary exposure.'

This was the kind of vote of confidence that Siya needed to hear, and it served as great motivation, but there was nothing to do but secure the thumb and let time work its healing magic on his hand. Once the initial shock had been absorbed, his management team took a decision. If Siya was going to be out of action for the rest of the season, it would make sense also to deal decisively with a niggling shoulder injury that had been worrying him. The procedure he had undergone when he first moved to Cape Town would be done on the other shoulder, and Siya could take the time to recover from both operations at once.

Everyone expected Siya to stay at home and relax while Western Province carried on with their Currie Cup campaign, but he had other ideas. For some time, he had been thinking

Leading the charge for the Grey High 2nd XV in a game against Port Alfred High. In Grade 10, Siya was still a few months away from a transformative growth spurt. (PRIVATE COLLECTION)

Siya and coach Dean Carelse pose with a cheetah during a photoshoot to announce his professional contract with the Free State rugby franchise, the Cheetahs. (PRIVATE COLLECTION)

The ten Grey High players, including Siya, selected for the 2008 Under-18 'A' Craven Week team pose with Old Boy Mike Catt (class of 1989, shown at right), who earned 75 caps for England and was part of the World Cup-winning team in 2003. Back row (from left): Shaun Potgieter, Craig Millson, Siyanda Mangaliso, Sikhokele Blom, Hayden de Villiers, Kurt Coleman and Zolani Faku. Kneeling (from left): Wade Lotter, Siya and Chuma Faas. (PRIVATE COLLECTION)

Siya tackles All Blacks centre Charlie Ngatai during the semi-final clash at the 2010 IRB Junior World Championship in Argentina. New Zealand won the game 36–7 and went on to win the tournament, with South Africa ending in third place. (TIM CLAYTON/CORBIS VIA GETTY IMAGES)

Warming up during a Western Province training session and press conference at the High Performance Centre in Bellville in August 2011. (CARL FOURIE/GALLO IMAGES)

Grey Old Boys JJ Engelbrecht and Siya Kolisi pose with Dean Carelse at a Springbok event at Grey High School in 2012. JJ had just made his Springbok debut against Argentina, and Siya had been invited to be part of the extended Springbok squad. (PRIVATE COLLECTION)

The DHL Stormers narrowly beat the Vodacom Bulls 19–14 in a Super Rugby clash on 2 June 2012. Here, Siya shows his speed and agility by evading both Flip van der Merwe and Werner Kruger in front of 50 000 fans at Loftus Versveld. (DOMINIC BARNARDT/GALLO IMAGES)

Siya is tackled by the Sharks' Tendai Mtawarira during the 2012 Super Rugby semi-final at Newlands. The Stormers lost 19–26 and were knocked out of the competition. (LUKE WALKER/GALLO IMAGES)

Siya poses with captain Jean de Villiers after his Springbok debut against Scotland at the Mbombela Stadium in Nelspruit. The Springboks won that game 30–17 and Siya was named man of the match.

(DUIF DU TOIT/GALLO IMAGES)

Siya's father, Fezakele Kolisi, proudly wearing his Stormers jersey during an interview at the home where Siya grew up on Mthembu Street in Zwide township.

(GALLO IMAGES/NETWERK 24/ LULAMA ZENZILE)

In action for the Stormers against the Brumbies at Newlands in the Super Rugby quarter-final on 20 June 2015. Cheslin Kolbe's single try wasn't enough and the Stormers lost 19–39.

Springbok coach Rassie Erasmus and newly appointed captain Siya Kolisi pose with the new caps Sibusiso Nkosi, RG Snyman and Aphiwe Dyantyi during a June 2018 Springbok media session.

Back at Emsengeni Primary School, where it all began, Siya looks on during a 2016 coaching session hosted by HCAT Rugby Goes Rural and Born Free Foundation Cat Sanctuary.
(CARL FOURIE/JAGUAR LAND ROVER/GALLO IMAGES)

Siya Kolisi, Tendai Mtawarira and Scarra Ntubeni during a Springbok training session at Cape Town Stadium on 1 June 2015. (ASHLEY VLOTMAN/GALLO IMAGES)

Siya and Rachel pose with their two children, Nicholas and Keziah, in Johannesburg, June 2018, shortly after he was named as Springbok captain.
(DAVID ROGERS/GETTY IMAGES)

In full flight for the Green and Gold.
(RICHARD HUGGARD/GALLO IMAGES)

about the fact that he had never gone through the Xhosa initiation ritual, which sees boys make the transition to manhood. He had contemplated going into the bush for the initiation straight after school but there had been too much at stake at that time. Then he had moved quickly through the ranks at the WPRI and into the senior team. And with the prospect of Springbok duty looming in his future, Siya realised that he would have even fewer opportunities to undergo initiation in the years ahead. He discussed it with Rachel and decided that this was the moment, so once the surgery was over and he was well enough, he packed his bags and headed off to the Eastern Cape to be part of the traditional Xhosa ritual.

The details of initiation are private, so virtually nothing is known about what Siya went through. He later told an interviewer: 'You go through so much there. You're alone, you can't sleep, you're sore and there's nothing you can do about it. You listen to the pain. And you think.'

In an article for *Africa Geographic* magazine, Richard Bullock describes the kind of ritual that Siya would have experienced, explaining how 'the initiates, who are known collectively as *abakhwetha*, or individually as *umkhwetha*, surrender their names. Their clothes are shredded in the days leading up to their exclusion, and they carry a short stick with a white cloth tied to one end. For three weeks, they exist outside of society, drinking almost no water and eating very little as they build up to the ceremonial circumcision and the period of recovery that follows it.'

At the end of it all, Rachel was there to greet Siya and welcome him back into society as a man. Their relationship continued to blossom during 2012, and it was obvious to everyone that they were good for each other. Rachel had grounded him and helped him grow into the kind of man he wanted to be. She had also gently introduced Siya to her Christian faith, and their regular church attendance had further deepened their relationship.

* * *

Siya got back to Cape Town just in time to see Province head off for the Currie Cup finals. They had managed to squeeze into the playoff rounds in third position and then defeat the Lions by 21 points to 16 to set up a final clash against the Sharks at Mr Price Kings Park Stadium. The home side was heavily favoured to win, not only because of all the injuries that Province were carrying but also because they hadn't won the competition since 2001.

Flyhalf Patrick Lambie gave the Sharks the lead with four well-taken penalties in the first half, but Juan de Jongh pulled one back for Province, scoring a try late in the first half with a brilliant sidestep around centre Lwazi Mvovo, and Province went ahead by 16 to 12.

That lead was cut down to one point straight after the break by another Lambie three-pointer, followed by another penalty, after Province failed to roll away, that put the Sharks ahead by 18 to 16. But the visitors kept their composure, and with 14 minutes to go, flyhalf Demetri Catrakilis set himself up perfectly on the 22-metre line and slotted a drop goal to take the score to 18–22.

Then, with five minutes to go, Province were again on the front foot and charging towards the line. Again, the ball was worked back to Catrakilis, who took the Sharks by surprise by moving to his left and attempting a left-footed drop kick that just crept over the crossbar for a further three points before the final whistle.

Western Province were crowned Currie Cup champions and the Sharks were forced to endure their third defeat in a final in three years. It was a bittersweet moment for Siya, who was unbelievably proud of his team but gutted that he had played such a minor role in the campaign due to injury.

Once again, the season came to an end without his achieving all his goals, and so he set his sights on playing for his country in 2013.

13

Green and Gold

If the Stormers had hoped that they were putting their injury problems behind them at the end of the 2012 season, they were very much mistaken. No one could have predicted that their inspirational captain, Schalk Burger, would be out of action for most of 2013, and nearly lose his life.

In March, Burger had had an MRI scan to see if he could address a persistent calf muscle problem. During the procedure, a cyst had been discovered growing on his spine, and it was decided that doctors would perform an operation to drain the cyst. While in hospital, Burger contracted a virus and began to experience severe headaches, nausea and convulsions. 'I didn't have a full seizure but it was close and I was seriously, seriously ill,' he told Independent Newspapers at the time. At one point, Schalk's family were called to the hospital because there was a real chance that he wasn't going to make it. The diagnosis was bacterial meningitis, and while it was touch and go for nearly a week, ultimately Burger pulled through. 'I was just unlucky to contract the bug but it's always a risk when you're cut open, I suppose.'

Nobody knew if he would ever play rugby again, but they

were certain that he wouldn't be doing anything for at least
the next three months. Siya felt terrible for Schalk and was
determined to fill the gap that his absence would leave.

* * *

One of the big events of the year for Siya had nothing to do
with rugby. During his 22nd year, he finally learned how to
drive, got his driving licence, and was rewarded with a car
sponsorship from one of South Africa's leading automotive
brands.

Siya's public profile grew steadily that year. There were
more fans, more publicity, more interest from sponsors and
a certainty that he was one to watch. Newspapers, radio stations and social media loved his feel-good backstory and his
romance with the beautiful blonde Rachel Smith, which was
still going strong.

Having a car brought Siya a new level of independence and
responsibility. He could see that it was time to move out of
communal living, after all these years sharing digs with
school friends and team-mates. Following his initiation, he
also felt ready to take on more responsibility, so he started to
look for a place of his own.

On the field, the Stormers lost the first two games of the season but then bounced back with two wins and a draw. But the
season never really got going and there was a lot of frustration in the team. They spent most of the season stuck below
tenth position on the log and finished seventh overall with 50
points, four points less than the Cheetahs, who were the low-
est-ranked team to make it into the qualifiers.

The disappointment of the Stormers' campaign quickly

gave way to the start of the Springbok season. The previous year, Siya had come agonisingly close to playing, but this year there would be no more excuses, no more waiting for his turn and talk of 'potential'. He wanted to make it happen, and he was gratified and relieved to be named on the bench for the national team against Scotland at Mbombela Stadium in Nelspruit. Of course, there was no guarantee he would play, but he was confident that he would get some game time.

The news media proudly shared the story with the nation and wrote gushingly about Siya's rags-to-riches journey from the streets of Zwide to the pinnacle of South African rugby. Everywhere he went, people came up to him and congratulated him on becoming a Springbok. Rachel was thrilled for him, naturally, as were many of his old coaches and teachers from high school. But there was something nagging at Siya, and it took him a while to figure out that he wanted to connect with his father and somehow to share the moment with him.

'He is going to be more emotional than me. I mean, I am the first Springbok from the township where I come from,' Kolisi told SuperSport.

Despite all the mentors, coaches, teachers and agents that Siya had had over the years, it was his dad who had first imparted the love of rugby to him, and he was determined both to honour that gift and to share his achievement with his father. The two men had lost touch over the years; life had taken them in very different directions and there was a lot of water under the bridge. They had simply drifted apart. But Siya never held any grudges against Fezakele. He remembered what he had been like when he was 18 years old and wondered what kind of a father he would have been at that age.

So, one evening, he called up his father and they spoke

about Siya's selection to the team. Obviously, as a rugby fan, Fezakele knew about it and they shared a few special moments acknowledging the achievement. Siya realised how little his dad had actually seen him play, so he spontaneously asked him if he would like to see the game in Nelspruit. Fezakele was delighted, but also a little daunted at the prospect of flying up to Mpumalanga. He had never travelled in an aircraft before.

Siya took a look at the schedules and realised that it was going to be a bit harder than just booking Fezakele a ticket, so he told SARU that he would be paying for it but would like their help in getting his father up to Nelspruit. The union was happy to oblige.

On 15 June 2013, one day before his son's 22nd birthday, Fezakele Kolisi took a flight from Port Elizabeth to Johannesburg, and then a connecting flight to Nelspruit to go and watch the Springboks play Scotland. 'He is going to be a very proud dad, and he is going to cry a bit and I will probably join him,' said Siya. The emotional reunion between Siya and his father at the ground before the game gave the event even more poignancy and importance than it would otherwise have had.

Both teams were missing some of their key players, the Springboks to injury and the Scots to the British Lions, who were on tour at the time. As a result, there were a lot of hungry young players on both sides, including Willie le Roux, Arno Botha and Trevor Nyakane in the starting lineup for the Boks.

Siya was nervous and distracted in the opening minutes of the game. Sitting on the bench, his mind was racing, and he kept looking around to see if he could spot his father. He swigged absent-mindedly at a bottle of water, then spat it out. It was a cold night in Nelspruit, but there was a passionate crowd all around them who were clearly delighted to host the Boks in their backyard.

Before he even had a chance to get comfortable on the bench, Siya found himself being called into the game. There was an early injury, and he heard assistant coach Johann van Graan telling him to get ready to play. Siya recalls how 'Van Graan quickly pulled me aside first, though, and just told me to forget everything because I had been struggling a bit in the week with getting to know all the new stuff. He just told me to do what I do, and every time I got the ball – and it came my way all day – I just ran with it.'

The reception from the crowd was loud and appreciative as Siya ran onto the field. It felt like they knew they were witnessing a moment in history. Eben Etzebeth ran over to tell him that the whole team had his back, and captain Jean de Villiers and Bryan Habana also took a moment to congratulate Siya. Then the game was on again and Siya got down to work.

The Scots were running hard at the Springboks with inventive lines and determined forward play. They kept the ball alive through multiple phases, working it gradually down the line until a gap opened up and they darted over for a try. Later on, Siya made a game-changing tackle when the Scottish lock, Jim Hamilton, broke through right in front of the posts. Siya lunged forward, managing to grab onto Hamilton's jersey, tug him back, and then extend into a perfect tackle that dropped the player on the spot. But, again, the Scots kept the ball alive and sent it all the way down to the wing for a second try in the corner.

Despite the Scottish onslaught, Siya was having a great game, carrying the ball aggressively and making big hits. When Adriaan Strauss emerged from an attacking line-out close to the Scots' try line, Siya latched in with him and they managed to make almost ten metres, leading a rolling maul that built and built before crashing over the line for a brilliant try.

They were down by four points at half-time. 'I remember at half-time, Jean said we have to score first in the second half to win this game,' recalls Siya. But Scotland had other ideas and a quick try at the beginning of the half took them into a 17–6 lead.

Siya felt a wave of panic and looked over at Jean de Villiers. He was surprised to see that the captain was laughing and assuring the players that it didn't matter, they were still going to win in the end. De Villiers was spot-on. The Springboks simply had too much class and depth, and they wore the Scots down, scoring twice in the last quarter of the match with a combination of great teamwork and individual brilliance.

The final score was 30–17 in favour of South Africa and Siya had notched up his first win in a senior Springbok jersey. 'After the game, I asked Jean why he was laughing,' Siya says. 'He just said that he couldn't show me how much he was panicking.' To make the night even sweeter, Siya was named man of the match. He was clearly proud of himself, but no one was prouder than Fezakele Kolisi as he watched his son perform with such courage and skill in front of the whole world.

As the year came to an end, all of South Africa grappled with the news that their beloved statesman Nelson Mandela had finally passed away. Before the new season kicked off, Siya wanted to pay homage to the man, so he went and got a small tattoo of Madiba's face on his shoulder blade that would be with him for as long as he lived.

14

Building a Family

Cape Town felt like home by 2014, but Siya never stopped going back to Port Elizabeth to visit. He loved giving back to the community where he had come from, and trying to inspire the young people who looked up to him as a Springbok, a Stormer and a local. Siya was only too glad to help when African Bombers needed new kit, he gave time and energy back to Emsengeni Primary School, and almost all of the teachers at Grey High School talk about the excitement and fun they have when Siya comes to visit.

Dean Carelse, the Grey High coach, remembers one visit in 2014 when Siya put on the Grey first-team kit and wandered around at a game, taking pictures with parents and students and even wandering into the stands to join in with the war cries he remembered so well. 'He even ran onto the field to play with the juniors, and there was nearly a riot,' laughs Carelse.

Driving around Zwide one afternoon, Siya was surprised to see a cousin he hadn't heard from for a long time. He pulled over to the side of the road and the two spent some time catching up. The cousin asked Siya if he was planning to visit his siblings. Siya was stunned and shook his head, and the man casually told him that they were living in an orphanage in the care of the state. After all these years with no clues, suddenly Siya had an address for them.

He was shaking with nervousness when he contacted the orphanage to find out about the two children. The answer came back that they were still there and would love to see their big brother. After that, things moved quickly and Siya made a plan to visit them the very next day. That night, as he later told *Men's Health* magazine, he dreamed about his mother, and in the dream, she told him 'that she wanted me to be there for them'.

The following morning, when Siya arrived at the orphanage, he was as nervous as he had been when he made his Springbok debut. He hoped that his younger brother would remember him from when they were kids, but he barely knew his younger sister; by the time she was born he was already out there living his life.

All the dreaming about the moment, all the projections about how it would be, ended the moment the door opened and Siya saw Liyema. The boy ran over and hugged his big brother so tightly that he nearly knocked the wind out of Siya. Then Liyema introduced his baby sister, Liphelo. She was a little more suspicious of Siya ... was he real? Would he stay or would he be just another adult who came and went and left them to fend for themselves? But Siya was happy to take some time and get to know the little girl, who had been through so much, and she felt it. Within a few minutes, she reached out to touch Siya's face and, in doing so, melted his heart.

'I knew right then that there was no way I was leaving without them,' says Siya. 'They were coming with me; I didn't care what it took. They were going to spend Christmas with me;

they were going to get the life and the family they always deserved.'

By the time Siya left the orphanage that day, the direction of his life had been altered forever. He was only 23, but he was determined that he would provide a better childhood for his two siblings than he had ever had. He didn't know how, and he didn't know what needed to happen, but he knew that he would be taking these two beautiful children with him to Cape Town as soon as possible and assuming responsibility for them.

Siya didn't know the exact procedure to be followed but he had a secret weapon in the form of Rachel. Once he told her what had happened, she was one hundred per cent on board and threw herself into the process of formally adopting the children. Siya was humble enough to realise that he couldn't do it without her, and the way she took on the system to make sure the children were with them by Christmas told him everything he needed to know about her.

Finally, when all the paperwork was done, Siya and Rachel drove to Port Elizabeth to collect the children and bring them home. On the way back to Cape Town, they spent a night in Knysna at the home of the Stormers physiotherapist, who had become a close personal friend. It was a profound culture shock for 12-year-old Liyema and 6-year-old Liphelo to be suddenly out of the system and in the care of two adults, but they adapted quickly. Siya remembered his own feelings of dislocation when he moved from Zwide to Grey Junior as a child, and he tried to help them manage the transition.

Over the course of a few days, Siya and Rachel went from being a carefree young couple to being parents, with all the responsibilities that entailed. By the end of 2013, they were living together and Rachel was in the process of quitting her marketing job. This meant she could focus on settling the kids and helping them adjust to their new lives in Cape Town. There was a lot of bureaucracy and admin involved, which to many people could have been overwhelming, but Rachel threw herself into the task and kept on pushing until she got results.

* * *

After the whirlwind of two new kids arriving in his life, Siya was left in no doubt that he could entrust the kids to Rachel, especially considering his new status and schedule as a Springbok meant he would be on the road more than ever. Following his debut against Scotland in June 2013, Siya had found himself back on the bench regularly for South Africa in that year's Rugby Championship. It was wonderful to be part of the setup, and to learn the ways of the Springboks, but what he wanted more than anything was to be part of the starting lineup.

Over the next few months, he played 16 minutes against Argentina in the first game, then 12 in the second, then 10 minutes against Australia and only 6 against New Zealand. It was valuable experience but he just wasn't able to deliver the kind of contribution he wanted to make to the national team. In early October 2013, he finally got some proper game time with 42 minutes on the park against the All Blacks in a game that South Africa lost 27–38.

With Liyema and Liphelo enrolled in schools in Cape Town at the beginning of 2014, Siya turned his focus to the upcoming Super Rugby season. The Stormers were determined to do better than they had the previous season, but they could not find a way to string together victories and build up momentum.

Time and again in 2014, the Stormers let their fans down, managing just two victories in the first ten rounds of the competition. Nobody thought it was good enough, and there was a palpable sense of frustration at the club. By July the team was languishing in 11th place overall, with no chance of making it into the qualifying rounds.

Siya was not happy with his form in 2014. He knew that he needed to work hard on his upper-body strength and to regain the explosive form that had seen him rise so quickly through the ranks. In October of that year, he told *News24* that his unhappiness started after a game against the Lions at Ellis Park in February: 'I had a really bad game, and from then I couldn't get up again.' It was bitterly disappointing but not really a surprise when he wasn't selected for the Springbok team to compete in the 2014 Rugby Championship in early August. There were six flankers in the squad: Schalk Burger, Willem Alberts, Oupa Mohojé, Francois Louw and Marcell Coetzee. All were great ball players, and all worthy Springboks.

There was nothing to do but just keep his head down, carry on working hard, and try and play himself back into form.

When the Currie Cup started later that year, Siya found his confidence returning. He was running well, stealing the ball at every opportunity and defending well too. It looked like the slump was behind him. In the *News24* interview, Siya admitted that he hadn't been enjoying his rugby that year. 'I just want to be positive and be happy,' he said, 'because I didn't really enjoy it this year. I took it too seriously.'

The other realisation that came in 2014 was that he needed to settle on one position and stake his claim to it without sacrificing any of his versatility. With so many good loose forwards competing for the limited Springbok places, he admitted that 'he can't be bouncing around all the loose forward positions', and needed to bulk up in the gym and specialise in a position, although that was hard to do with different coaches wanting different things from their loose forwards.

* * *

The Currie Cup started off well, and Western Province dominated in every game they played, winning five out of five games. Siya's faith in himself and in his abilities came streaming back.

Then, in Round Six, Western Province travelled up to Johannesburg to take on the Golden Lions. They were riding the crest of a wave that they felt certain would sweep them all the way into the final. They had already beaten the Lions 27–14 in Round Three, so they were confident that they would carry on in the same fashion, although Ellis Park was fast becoming some kind of hoodoo ground for them. The Stormers had lost there earlier in the year, in a humiliating 10–34 drubbing in February, and every time there was a big game at Ellis Park, it felt like something went wrong. Still, Western Province had lost only once in the last 21 games they had played, so this should have been no different.

How wrong they were. The Lions were in a dominant mood on that day. Initially, Province fought their way up to a 19–14 lead, but then the Lions pack clawed their way back, led by the hooker Akker van der Merwe, who had a superb game. In the second half, the Lions ran in three tries in 15 minutes, and forced the visitors to miss over 30 tackles – unheard of in a team that prided itself on its defence. The final score was 35 to 19 in favour of the Lions.

For most of the game, Siya was a spectator. In the eighth minute, his world came crashing down around him when he tore the medial collateral ligaments in both of his knees. It was the kind of injury that would heal with four to six weeks' rest, but coming at a time when he was playing so well and once again staking a claim to a place in the Bok team, it was a crushing blow. He set himself the goal of making it back into the Western Province team for the qualifiers at the end of the season, but that didn't happen and he was forced, once again, to watch from the sidelines as his team made it to the finals and got their revenge against the Lions with a 19–16 victory at Newlands on 25 October.

Of course, Siya was thrilled for his team-mates and for his club, but he was worried that injuries were always going to keep him from what should be the biggest games of his career. It was frustrating but he managed to stay focused on healing his body and strengthening his body and mind.

* * *

On the field, there was nothing for him to do but wait, but in the rest of his life, it was time for some action. Seeing Rachel with Liyema and Liphelo was a great joy to him, and she was proving herself to be as courageous and determined as any team-mate he had ever played alongside. Her commitment to him and to her 'kids', as she already thought of them, was profoundly gratifying, and it fulfilled something deep in Siya that had been missing ever since his childhood.

Growing up, he had never had a real home of his own. He had been welcomed in dozens of homes around the country, but always as a guest or a visitor. Creating a home with Rachel

138

was a tremendously healing process for him. Of course, he had loved his time in digs with his rugby brothers and his school friends, but those days were over and he was thriving on a renewed sense of purpose and mission towards his family.

The couple used to tease one another about which of them was the more romantic, and they would often set up elaborate dates and outings together, so it was no surprise to Rachel when 'he came home from training one day with a huge bunch of flowers and made me breakfast in bed, and told me to pack a bag'. She thought that he had probably booked a hotel for the night, but in fact they went straight off to a helipad for a helicopter trip over Cape Town. It was the first time either of them had been in a helicopter, and Siya was having second thoughts by the time they finally took off.

'Siya was freaking out. His hands were sweating and shaking,' Rachel told *City Press*. But there was no turning back, so they climbed in and held on tight as the chopper took off. The views were spectacular, and were almost enough to cancel out the butterflies that were churning in Siya's stomach, both from the helicopter trip and from the engagement ring he was carrying in his pocket.

'We're going to crash. This thing is going to fall,' he told himself.

Up there above the clouds, looking out over the city that had embraced him, and that he had been proud to represent for the last three years, Siya pulled out the ring and proposed to Rachel. He was 'shaking like a leaf', but she accepted. In the video taken by the pilot, you can see Rachel laughing with delight as Siya puts the ring on her finger, and then they fall into one another's arms and kiss in a classic fairy-tale moment.

They couldn't wait to tell Liyema and Liphelo, and upon seeing their reactions to the news, Siya knew immediately he had made the right choice for a wife.

Rachel was under no illusions about the difficulty of being married to an international rugby player who was travelling around the world for months at a time. 'It is not so normal trying to raise children with someone constantly travelling. And it's tough to just stay at home. But these are sacrifices I have decided to make,' she told *City Press*. But she was also quick to acknowledge that they had been blessed by the opportunities that rugby had given them, including the means to bring up two children. 'Rugby has always been a part of Siya. It came before all of us – me and the kids.'

The family spent a happy December together, secure in the knowledge that they were committing themselves to a life together. As 2015 rolled around and thoughts turned to the new season, Rachel and Siya were delighted to find out that they could expect their first child in September of that year.

* * *

The mantle of responsibility settled a little heavier on Siya's shoulders as the year kicked off, but he felt ready for it and looked forward to an amazing year. His goal for 2015 was a simple one: to play for the Springboks at the Rugby World Cup in England. The way to make sure that happened was to stay fit and healthy, and to have the kind of Super Rugby season that he'd been striving to achieve for the last four years.

Siya felt confident that the injuries to his knees were healed and that he was ready to give his everything to the challenges ahead. Everyone could see that on paper this Stormers squad had nothing to fear from any of the other teams in the Super Rugby competition. With Allister Coetzee as coach and Duane Vermeulen as captain, the team was settled and well balanced. Players like Schalk Burger, Nizaam Carr, Bongi Mbonambi and Eben Etzebeth in the pack and Kurt Coleman, Damian de Allende and Juan de Jongh in the back row were all fit and raring to go, and a massive wave of support was growing in Cape Town. In fact, by the end of the season, the average attendance for a Stormers game at Newlands stood at over 40 000, far higher than the second-highest total, which was 26 000 for the Bulls.

Finally, Siya was able to put in the kind of great season that he'd been aspiring to for years. The season kicked off with a 29–17 defeat of the Bulls, followed by victory over the Blues a few weeks later that left the Stormers on top of the overall standings with eight points. In both of those games, Siya came on with 20 minutes to play and quickly showed his worth. This led to regular selection in the starting lineup, which was exactly what Siya wanted.

By the end of the regular season, Siya had played in every Stormers game, and he was still hungry for more. His body was responding well, and he was certain that he would be back in contention for the Springbok team travelling to the World Cup.

The Stormers finished top of the South African Conference, third overall, and were drawn to play the Brumbies in the first of the quarter-finals. But all their hopes of Super Rugby glory came crashing down in the face of a six-try onslaught from the Canberra side. On the day, the Brumbies were simply unstoppable, and winger Joe Tomane scored three in the first half hour of the game. A single try from Cheslin Kolbe early in the second half gave the home fans something to cheer about, but it was too little, too late. In the end, the Brumbies handed the Stormers a 19–39 defeat, and their season was once again cut short before they could go all the way.

In the semi-final, the Brumbies were beaten by the Hurricanes, who went on to lose in the final against the Highlanders. All attention turned to the upcoming World Cup and the team selection, but not in the Kolisi household. They had far more important things to think about.

Exhibiting the impeccable timing that his father showed on the rugby field, baby Nicholas Kolisi was born early in September, right between the Super 15 season and the Rugby World Cup, which meant that Siya was at home, available and very much involved in the life-changing birth of his son.

Of course, he was already used to being responsible for two youngsters, and he thrived on it, but having a newborn in the house took things to a whole new level. No doubt it brought back memories of his own childhood, when Liyema came to live with him and his grandmother in Mthembu Street. It certainly kept him from worrying too much about the upcoming announcement of the World Cup squad.

Siya thought he had done enough, but there were so many great loose forwards in contention that he wasn't certain of securing a place in the Springbok squad. Duane Vermeulen, Oupa Mohojé, Francois Louw, Schalk Burger, Heinrich Brüssow ... they were all fantastic players who could walk into most international teams, to say nothing of Marcell Coetzee and Willem Alberts as well.

So, when the big announcement finally came, Siya was absolutely delighted to be named to the squad of 31 players by coach Heyneke Meyer, along with Duane Vermeulen, Pieter-Steph du Toit, Francois Louw and Schalk Burger.

* * *

For the 2015 Rugby World Cup, South Africa was drawn in Pool
B, along with Scotland, Japan, Samoa and the United States.
The first Pool B game pitted the Springboks against Japan
at the Brighton Community Stadium on 19 September. Siya
was once again on the bench for this game. South Africa had
never lost to Japan in their history, so they were confident
going into the encounter, despite the fact that the Japanese
were being coached by the wily Australian Eddie Jones, who
had shown his confidence earlier in the week. Jones had commented ominously that this 'could be a day to remember for
Japanese rugby', but the loyal South African rugby public dis-
missed that as mere hype.

The Springboks started the first game of the World Cup well,
running good lines at the Cherry Blossoms and keeping the
ball alive through a number of phases, but when Japan finally
won a turnover, they countered strongly. 'There's already a
real intensity from both teams,' said TV commentator Joel
Stransky, as it became obvious that Japan were no longer con-
tent to be seen as pushovers.

Surprisingly, Japan were first on the scoreboard with
a penalty in the eighth minute, but ten minutes later the
Boks responded well with a rolling maul from the five-metre
line. Francois Louw tucked the ball up safely and the pack
steamed forward over the line for a try, which Patrick Lambie
converted.

But the Japanese forwards were not overawed by the
Springbok pack. They came back hard at them, testing their
defences again and again, and only five minutes after Francois
Louw's try they were on the board after a ten-man rolling

maul saw them crash over the line, much to the delight of the local crowd and to the neutrals who had quickly gotten behind the underdogs.

It was 12–10 at the break, and the Springboks had been forced to accept that this was not the kind of Japanese team they were used to playing against. The Cherry Blossoms had been reengineered to play at the highest level, and they demanded respect. Early in the second half, the Boks began to assert the kind of dominance they were used to, and they moved further ahead when Lood de Jager grabbed the ball like it was a cricket ball, broke through the Japanese defensive line, and charged off alone to score a try under the posts.

But Japan didn't relent for a second, backed up by a crowd that was now fully behind them, and a string of successful penalty kicks from Ayumu Goromaru put the two teams level at 19 apiece. In the 57th minute, Siya got his chance when he came on to replace Pieter-Steph du Toit, and he immediately swung into action for the team. The noise in the stadium was deafening and the crowd roared every time Japan got the ball. More fresh legs were needed, and so Adriaan Strauss came on for Bismarck du Plessis. In the 61st minute the score was 22–22 when Strauss gathered the ball like an inside centre, beat two men, executed a beautiful sidestep, and sprinted over the line.

But the game was far from over, and the Japanese backline came to the party in a big way with ten minutes left to play. They executed a textbook backline try that saw the backs threading the needle, finding space, and releasing each player at just the right moment. 'Perfectly orchestrated, clinical in its execution, Goromaru capitalised on the outside,' said the commentators, and the game was tied again. Then in the 72nd minute, Handre Pollard kicked the Boks three points clear, although from the way the crowd was chanting for Japan, you would be forgiven for thinking they were ahead.

With four minutes to go, Japan built a movement from their own 22-metre line, somehow willing the ball forward in wave after wave. Seven phases later and they had found their way to the Springboks' 22-metre line with three minutes to the final whistle. Ten phases, then eleven phases and they inched forward, stalking for a try as the exhausted Boks defended with everything they had. Eighteen phases, two minutes to play, and you could barely hear yourself think in the stadium as the Japanese worked the ball up to the five-metre line. There was a huge surge and it was nearly over, but the Japanese were heroically held up by Fourie du Preez. Bodies were scattered everywhere when the whistle went and the ref showed a yellow card to Coenie Oosthuizen. The Japanese huddled, discussing their options, refining their strategy, and catching their breath while the Springboks looked on uneasily, aware that momentum was firmly against them.

Japan opted for a line-out with one minute to go.

They won the ball and simply willed it over the line, where it disappeared under a giant cluster of exhausted bodies. The ref couldn't decide, but eventually it seemed that Siya had the ball in his possession and the try was averted.

But still the contest wasn't over, and a scrum on the five-metre line led to another Japanese penalty. At 32–29 to the Boks, they could have taken the three-point penalty and earned a very respectable draw, but no ... they were going for a win and one of the biggest upsets in the history of sport. Another scrum. The clock ticked past 80 minutes ... then a reset and they had it again, launching attackers at the Springbok line, which was holding fast ... until finally the ball was worked all the way out towards the right. Only a great tackle from Adriaan Strauss prevented the try in the corner of the field.

Then came the switch, the ball flew out to the left, and suddenly space opened up, an overlap for Japan. The ball landed in the hands of Karne Hesketh, who had just come on to provide some fresh legs, and he powered over the line for a try to take Japan two points clear of the Boks.

There was pandemonium in the stadium as the final whistle blew. The Springboks had lost to Japan for the first time ever.

In *For the Record*, Gary Teichmann describes 'the stillness in a defeated Springbok dressing room. No one talks. No one offers a wry smile or curses their luck. There is a stunned silence, of big men staring blankly at the ever-increasing pile of dirty kit.'

Nobody who wasn't there can know what it was like in the change room after that game against Japan, but it must have been uncomfortable, to say the least. The BBC called it 'the biggest upset in rugby union history', and the South African press were scathing about the Springbok team's performance, the management and their prospects for the rest of the tournament. It was a dark time to be part of the Springbok setup, but one of the blessings of being on a carefully managed tour far from home is that the players are shielded from most of the media, as well as from the legions of armchair coaches who phone in to talk-radio stations, offering unwanted advice and wringing their hands in despair about the state of the national team.

Global sports tournaments thrive on big drama, and there is always a new talking point around the corner, so after a few days things got back to normal and the team's self-confidence returned with impressive wins against Samoa (46–6), then Scotland (34–16) and a 64–0 dismantling of the United States.

Siya got to play for only 34 minutes in total during that World Cup, but he had an amazing time with the team, travelling around and soaking in the experience. At some point during the tournament, Rachel flew to England with her newborn baby and joined the Springbok tour. 'It was a great experience for me,' Siya told *Sport24* after the tournament. 'I had a great time with the guys that weren't playing and the guys that were playing as well … my family was there for a bit so it was amazing.'

The Springboks finished top of Pool B, despite their historic loss to Japan, and were drawn against Wales in the first quarter-final of the tournament. In front of 75 000 screaming fans at Twickenham, the two sides treated the crowd to a fantastic sporting spectacle. The lead constantly changed as both kickers kept the scoreboard active with penalties and drop kicks. With seven minutes left to play, the score was 18–16 to Wales and they were hanging onto the lead with everything they had. Then the Springboks won a scrum, which held up, then wheeled a little to the right. Duane Vermeulen spotted an opportunity, picked up the ball, and made for the corner, drawing defenders towards him before offloading beautifully to Fourie du Preez, who dived over the line unopposed to make it 23–19.

In the dying moments of the game, Patrick Lambie attempted a drop kick, which fell short. Wales gathered up the ball and ran at the Springboks in desperate waves to try and claw their way back in, but the Springbok defensive lines held on and the team recorded a hard-earned victory and a place in the semi-finals.

On the same day, New Zealand cruised easily past France, beating them by 62 points to 13 and setting up a date with the Springboks.

The semi-final on 24 October proved to be the end of the road for South Africa. The team gave their all against the All Blacks in a relentlessly physical encounter. They forced their opponents into giving away multiple penalties, but it wasn't enough on the day. Five penalties from Handre Pollard and one from Lambie late in the game kept the Springboks in it until the very end, and they were up at half-time, but tries from Beauden Barrett and flanker Jerome Kaino took the game out of reach for South Africa and they went down 18–20. They were knocked out and forced to watch as the All Blacks went on to beat Australia in the final and retain the title of world champions.

Part 3

15

Storm Clouds Gather

The 2016 Super Rugby season kicked off in February with a revised format. No longer would the competition be restricted to teams from Australia, New Zealand and South Africa. Now there would also be games against the Jaguares from Argentina and Japan's Sunwolves. The Southern Kings from the Eastern Cape were also back in contention, taking the total number of teams in the competition up to 18.

With 142 matches scheduled for the competition, the season was going to be longer than ever, running well into July, including a break during June for scheduled international matches, so management of the players and their bodies was more important than ever.

There had been some changes at the Stormers, too, during the off-season. Coach Allister Coetzee had accepted an offer to coach in Japan for the Kobelco Steelers, otherwise known as the Kobe Steel Rugby Club. 'We tried our best to keep Allister,' said Western Province director of rugby Gert Smal in a press release. 'Not only is he a fantastic coach but we have a great relationship – on and off the field.'

But the dismay at losing Coetzee was soon replaced by

elation as the management team announced that they had
secured the services of the decorated international coach
Eddie Jones. Having coached the Wallabies between 2001 and
2007, Jones had also been a technical advisor to the Springboks
when they won the World Cup in 2007. Most recently, he had
been the guiding hand behind Japan's shock victory over the
Springboks at the 2015 World Cup, so everyone was keenly
aware of his tactical genius and coaching ability. It was a
great coup for the Stormers to attract him to their franchise.
'Our director of rugby always promised that he would deliver
the best and in Eddie Jones I am more than satisfied that we
have appointed the best coach to take over the reins of the
DHL Stormers,' said Thelo Wakefield, president of the Western
Province Rugby Football Union.

Jones would be working with former Springbok centre
Robbie Fleck as his attack coach, and former SA Sevens coach
Paul Treu as his defence coach. It looked set to be a winning
combination. 'I am well aware of the responsibilities that
come with this job, one of the biggest franchise jobs in world
rugby, but I am also excited about the talent available in the
DHL Stormers squad and the potential of this playing squad,'
said Jones.

The squad was in fantastic shape heading into the 2016 season. Frans Malherbe, Eben Etzebeth and Siya, all graduates of
the famous WPRI class of 2010, had been retained on long-term
contracts, alongside the explosive back Damian de Allende.
And the up-and-coming star Pieter-Steph du Toit was also
joining the team from the Sharks, which was a tremendous
coup for the team.

Jones arrived in Cape Town towards the end of 2015, after
the Rugby World Cup had wrapped up. He told the media at a

press conference that he wasn't interested in changing the DNA of the team. He was going to introduce some new ideas of his own but he wanted 'the Stormers to carry on being the Stormers', and he was relishing the idea of developing a new leadership group at Western Province. Many of the stalwarts who had done so much for rugby in Cape Town, such as Jean de Villiers and Schalk Burger, were coming to the end of their playing careers and it was time for younger players to take up the mantle and lead the club.

There was only one cloud in this otherwise perfect sky and the promise of an incredible season for the Stormers. The England coaching position had recently become vacant with the departure of Stuart Lancaster, and Eddie Jones's name immediately joined the list of potential replacements. But Jones was resolute that he was going to stay in Cape Town: 'I'm committed to the Stormers. This morning, I woke up and saw Table Mountain and said, "I'm here."'

That cloud on the horizon very quickly turned into a storm cloud. Within two weeks of his arrival, Jones had changed his mind and was on a plane back to the UK to take over as head coach of the England rugby team. It was a devastating blow to the Stormers players and to every rugby-loving Capetonian, especially with the start of the new season just a couple of weeks away. But, once the dust settled, Cape Town rugby fans began to come to terms with his departure. After all, coaching England was arguably the most prestigious job in world rugby, and it hadn't been available when Jones signed for the Stormers. The timing was bad, and he was breaking his contract, but few coaches would not have jumped at such an opportunity.

Robbie Fleck was promoted to the job of Stormers head

coach, and the first training camp of the season was scheduled for 12–16 January in Wilderness. The former Springbok centre had been a Cape rugby stalwart since his schoolboy days, and he was perfectly suited to take over the position. He had enjoyed a great 2015 as coach of the Under-21s, who had lost only one game all season, and he was already well integrated into the system. Once the furore over Eddie Jones died down, the team was able to focus again and pick up where they had left off.

Any misgivings that the fans may have had were soon extinguished with two solid victories in the first two games of the season, including a 33–9 dismantling of the Blue Bulls at Newlands. All in all, the Stormers won ten of their fifteen games in the regular season, ending up third overall and only one point behind the Lions in the South African Conference.

Before the knockout rounds began in July, the competition took a break to accommodate the international fixtures, and South African rugby fans found themselves looking forward to a three-match tour from the Irish, who hadn't been to South Africa since 2004.

* * *

Things change fast in world rugby. Allister Coetzee had jetted off to Japan in October but by April he had been called back and installed as the new Springbok coach. Suddenly, the chopping and changing that had marked the Eddie Jones episode seemed par for the course. Coetzee made his first team selection on 28 May, a few weeks before the series against Ireland kicked off.

Siya was named among the Springboks, and he was thrilled

when Scarra Ntubeni also got the call-up to join the Bok squad. He had come so close so many times, and Siya desperately wanted to see his old friend running out into a stadium wearing the Springbok jersey. He had been part of the squad three times and had been seriously considered for the 2015 World Cup squad, until at the last minute Heyneke Meyer selected Schalk Brits as his backup hooker. Everyone knew Scarra was good enough to be a Springbok, but in a country with so much rugby talent, often it's a question of timing, injury and sheer luck when it comes to crossing that final hurdle into the elite 15.

But, when the final team lineup was announced, the hooker position went to Bongi Mbonambi, who had had an amazing season. He had played more than twice as much rugby as Scarra had during that season's Super Rugby tournament. It had been a tough choice for the coach, and he'd understandably gone with the Bulls man.

Although the team hadn't played together since the World Cup, and despite the fact that it was the new coach's first game in charge, the Springboks were expected to win against Ireland. After all, the Irish had never beaten them on home soil.

Siya had come on as a substitute 13 times for the Boks. Many people felt that he had earned a place in the starting lineup in the upcoming game against Ireland, and this time around the new coach agreed. At Newlands on 11 June, five days before he turned 25, Siya started his first game for South Africa, and played the full 80 minutes of a hard-fought battle. It was also the debut match for the lively and impressive scrumhalf Faf de Klerk, who was expected to play a crucial role for the Boks in the years ahead.

But the Boks' discipline let them down in the early phases

of the game, and this allowed Ireland to settle quickly and get some early points on the board, thanks to a cheeky chip over the defence by Luke Marshall that let Jared Payne in for a try.

The Springboks never really got going, even when Ireland's CJ Stander received a red card in the middle of the first half and another of their players was sin-binned. The Irish finished the first half with only 13 men on the field, yet somehow were able to pull ahead early in the second half.

In the closing moments of the game, Ireland were leading by 26–20 and the Springboks threw everything they had at the tourists. It almost seemed like JP Pietersen had rescued the game in the dying seconds of the 80th minute with a try in the corner, but three defenders just managed to bundle him into touch in the nick of time and it was all over. Ireland had beaten South Africa in South Africa for the first time.

It was a big disappointment to lose the opening game, but the team recovered well to record wins in the next two games. Siya was pleased to start in both of those games, alongside Francois Louw at blindside flanker and Duane Vermeulen in the number 8 jersey.

* * *

No sooner were the internationals finished than the Super Rugby competition resumed. Going into the quarter-finals, Robbie Fleck's team were confident that home-ground advantage would help them overcome the Chiefs, who would have to travel from New Zealand for the game on 23 July.

It was not to be. The home team got off to the worst start possible when Siya damaged the ligaments in his left ankle in the third minute of the game and had to leave the field. He was devastated. After starting in every single game of the season, and contributing so much, once again he would miss the last few knock-out games and the final – if the Stormers made it all the way.

A minute after he left the field, the Chiefs slotted their first penalty and it was 3–0. After that, the Stormers were never really in it. That night, the Chiefs were playing in a different class, attacking from all angles, being creative in their choices yet rock-solid on defence. In the end, they ran in eight tries past the embattled Stormers defence while Siya looked on unhappily from the sidelines.

The Chiefs were up by 34–13 at half-time, and by the end had extended their lead to 60–21. It was an emphatic display to which the Stormers had no reply. Siya was convinced that he would have had an impact on the game and that his injury so early on made all the difference, but there was nothing anyone could do except suck it up and move on.

The ankle injury was worse than he had feared, and Siya was forced to undergo surgery the following week. He would be out of action for three months and would miss the upcoming Rugby Championship, which was due to get under way with a game against Argentina in Nelspruit in early August. But, lying in the hospital bed after a successful operation to repair the ankle ligaments, Siya reflected on the fact that there were thousands of fans out there wishing him a speedy recovery and that meant a lot to him. He chose to look on the bright side, figuring that it would give him more time at home to focus on preparations for his upcoming wedding.

Being forced to take it easy and give his ankle time to recover meant there was plenty of time for sitting around and watching the Springboks compete in the Rugby Championship. The results were worrying for Allister Coetzee and the general public. Again and again, the Springboks came up short against the competition. They narrowly beat Argentina at home, then lost to them for the first time ever in the return match, lost again in Australia, and were hammered by the All Blacks 57 points to 15.

Alarm bells were ringing in the upper management of the team, and there was a lot of pressure to ensure a good end-of-year tour. Siya knew he would be fit by then, and he was determined to be an integral part of a Springbok revival. In the meantime, there was the urgent matter of a wedding to take care of.

* * *

Siya and Rachel had imagined their wedding day hundreds of times since their engagement. None of the scenarios they envisaged involved Siya walking up the aisle on crutches wearing a controlled ankle motion boot, also known as a 'moon boot', to protect his ankle. But that was the reality, and so they just rolled with it.

There was a threat of rain hanging over the Cape Winelands that weekend in August 2016, but it did nothing to dampen the excitement at the MolenVliet Oosthuizen Family Vineyards as the big day dawned. Siya had asked Nick Holton to be his best man, while team-mates like Scarra, Nizaam and Eben were among the groomsmen. There was plenty of playful banter and teasing as the men gathered hours before the ceremony and got dressed. Siya wore a regal deep-blue tuxedo that contrasted nicely with his groomsmen, who were wearing classic black suits with white shirts.

Rachel's dress had been designed by Jenny le Roux and the team at Habits Fashion in Claremont. They had created a stunning gown complete with French Chantilly lace and Italian jewels. The white gown contrasted with the sleek black dresses worn by Rachel's bridesmaids, and the symbolism of black and white coming together in a joyous occasion was lost on no one.

Liyema, Liphelo and little Nicholas were super-excited and they charged around the wedding venue in their custom-fitted suits. 'It's a big step forward for all of us,' Rachel told the TV magazine show *Top Billing*. 'It'll be good for them and bring more security to their lives.'

The 200 guests crammed into a small old wine cellar, with oak barrels lining one wall, and waited for the bride to make her entrance as the rain fell outside. Siya had always been good at keeping his emotions in check on the playing field, but when he saw his bride walking towards him, something inside him cracked open and he struggled to keep it together. There were tears all around as Rachel's dad walked her down the aisle and the ceremony began.

'Siya's not normally an emotional guy,' Eben told the TV journalists, 'but I think seeing the love of your life coming down the aisle – any man will get emotional.'

The ceremony was beautiful and so was the party afterwards. Everyone could see the love and commitment that the couple felt towards one another and it infused the weekend with warmth and happiness. This was one of the few times that Siya was able to bring all the elements of his life together – his family from Zwide, his school friends and his teammates from Western Province and the Springboks, as well as Rachel and the whole Smith family. The best part for Siya was 'seeing friends and family come together, people who've never met before, and for my brother and sister to see what this life is about, which is something I never had.' Many of the guests stayed the whole weekend and partied with Siya and Rachel into the early hours of the morning, watching as he tried his best to half-dance with one good leg.

The wedding was big news all over the country. For better or worse, everyone was interested in the Kolisi wedding. As a multiracial couple in a country still struggling to reconcile its feelings about race, Siya and Rachel began to attract comment from the best and the worst of people. Rachel was on the receiving end of some truly hateful comments, but she took it all in her stride and coped in her usual no-nonsense way.

16

Personal Highs, Professional Lows

The 2016 end-of-year tour was a chance to get the Springboks back on a good footing after a difficult campaign. Their first step on the road to redemption was against the Barbarians on 5 November at Wembley Stadium.

Many of the first-choice players were unavailable due to injury, which gave coach Allister Coetzee a chance to blood some new young players who had impressed during the regular season. With Francois Louw, Duane Vermeulen and Siya all recovering from injuries, the team included Roelof Smit from the Blue Bulls and the Sharks' Jean-Luc du Preez.

On the day, the Springboks gave it everything they had but left the impression that Springbok rugby was not in a good place. They battled hard to earn a 31–31 draw, but the Barbarians, consisting mostly of Super Rugby players who were not yet full internationals, looked like a team who were out for a good time and had barely bothered to practise before the match. Rohan Janse van Rensburg saved the game for the Boks with a late try, but Patrick Lambie was unable to convert and they had to settle for a draw instead.

After the game, Britain's *Guardian* newspaper wrote: 'For

all the pyrotechnics, the impression that South African rugby is in a desperate place was not alleviated by this,' and went on to say that this display from the Springboks 'did not bode well for the rest of the autumn'.

The writer of the piece, Michael Aylwin, was spot-on. The next few weeks brought the lowest points that Springbok rugby had ever plumbed. England beat the Boks for the first time since 2006, recording four tries against the Springboks' two to win 37–21 at Twickenham. The Springboks seemed to lack leadership on the field, they made way too many unforced errors, and their discipline was weak. If it hadn't been for a late try in the corner from Willie le Roux, the scoreline would have looked much less respectable than it did.

Still, the tour trundled on with a trip to Italy and a chance to gain some momentum. The Boks had never lost to the Italians, who were ranked 13th in the world, and everyone expected the South Africans to win comfortably.

But this was not the Italy that South Africa was used to facing. They had a new Irish coach, Conor O'Shea, who had adopted a back-to-basics approach and introduced some aggressive attacking tactics. The Italians discovered a new belief in themselves, and when they came up against a Bok team that was low in confidence, it soon became apparent that a Springbok victory was by no means a certainty.

The two teams met at Florence's Stadio Artemio Franchi on 19 November. Bryan Habana scored early for the Boks, but a string of wayward passes, dropped balls and ineffective mauls let the Italians back into the match with a try from the South African-born Andries van Schalkwyk. The Boks went ahead again thanks to Damian de Allende, but the Azzurri evened the score 15–15 through the efforts of winger Giovanbattista

Venditti, and then went two points ahead following the conversion.

Both teams were able to put over one more penalty each, but that was enough for Italy to record a famous 20–18 victory over South Africa. The Italians were beside themselves with joy while South Africa was despondent. 'We're at an all-time low,' commented Jean de Villiers to SuperSport, while captain Adriaan Strauss apologised to the nation, noting, 'We are in a dark place at the moment and we must get ourselves out of it.'

Allister Coetzee was well aware that this defeat could cost him his job. After the game, he said: 'We are not going to offer any excuses, what happened today was not worthy of what we stand for as a team and as a rugby-playing country.' But it didn't seem like he had any answers to stop the rot.

The optimists in the country were probably hoping for a fairy-tale comeback against Wales in the final game of the tour, at Cardiff's Principality Stadium on 26 November, but it was not to be. Wales were a completely different prospect to Italy, and the Springboks managed to get only 13 points on the board, thanks to two penalties from Elton Jantjies and a late try from Uzair Cassiem, converted by Patrick Lambie. Wales, on the other hand, scored two tries and 17 points with the boot.

The final score was 27–13 and the Springbok team returned home humbled and in disarray. Fans and commentators began lining up to lambaste this as the worst Springbok team of all time, and they were merciless in their criticism of the players, the coach and the whole structure of South African rugby. Former coach Nick Mallett summed it all up in a tweet: 'SA rugby is in a dreadful, dreadful state.'

* * *

For Siya, watching the Springboks stumble from defeat to defeat was almost as hard as having to watch from the sidelines for a full six months. Something had to change.

The first few weeks of February 2017 marked the end of a nearly six-month layoff from rugby. Siya hadn't played a competitive game since 23 July 2016. It had been by far the longest time that he had been sidelined from the game he loved and that had shaped his life. With the 2017 Super Rugby season looming, he was raring to go and to make up for lost time.

There had been many stages on the road to recovery since the game in July. After the operation came the first few weeks of total rest, followed by rehab to restore joint flexibility in the ankle and build up the load so that the soft tissue could handle it, as well as working on strength and conditioning. Siya was fortunate that he had spent his whole professional career in one franchise. The Western Province medical team knew his body, understood what it could and could not handle, and were able to devise a tailor-made recovery plan.

By the time the Super Rugby season kicked off in 2017, Siya was ready. This was the first season he would be playing as a married man, as a father and as a Springbok. Everything had come together over the last few years and everyone could see the boy he once was had grown up and become a man.

Of course, his playful, fun-loving side was as strong as ever, but there was a new maturity and stability in the way he carried himself on and off the field that impressed his growing legion of fans. Siya had really connected with the public, he'd grown a huge following, and he was fit and ready to play. The good news kept on coming, and the couple were overjoyed when they found out that Rachel was pregnant again and they were going to welcome another child into the home towards the end of the year.

Rachel used her Instagram account to tell all of her followers the exciting news in her own humorous way. She wrote in an ironic post, 'Halfway in and looking forward to all the joys parenting brings: a baby that actually burps and doesn't vomit everywhere in the process, sleeps through the night and never requires sleep training' ... the list of parental disruptions went on and on and gave the impression that the family were dealing with the whirlwind of having young children and balancing busy careers at the same time.

Siya was grateful to his wife for all the extra time that she put into the family when he was away on tour. As Rachel's pregnancy developed, the Super Rugby season got going.

Once again, 18 teams would do battle in the extended format, with the Hurricanes defending their title for the first time. No South African team had won the Super Rugby title since the Bulls in 2010, and there was an expectation that the Stormers, who featured such a stellar group of players, would make South Africa proud. The members of the WPRI class of 2010 were mature now, they were mostly still together in one team, and they were playing some of the best rugby of their lives. Robbie Fleck had been retained as Stormers coach and had settled in after being thrust unexpectedly into the position at the beginning of the previous season. Fleck was looking forward to the new season. He had gone on fact-finding missions to rugby clubs around the world and was pushing himself to be a better coach since the harrowing defeat by the Chiefs in the 2016 finals. 'Last year I started out on the back foot,' Fleck told SuperSport before the first match of the season, 'but this time I know I have buy-in from the players, and they have confidence in me. I am in a far better spot than I was last year.'

The 45-man squad was a good balance of youth and

experience, and was to be captained by Juan de Jongh. There were five players under 21 and double that number who had played over 50 games of Super Rugby. Siya could look around him and see players that he had known and trusted for years: guys like Kurt Coleman, who had been in the team with him at Grey; Frans Malherbe, Nizaam Carr and Eben Etzebeth, who had been on the journey with him; and Pieter-Steph du Toit and Damian Willemse, who had joined the team and made such a difference in the last few years.

'Everyone has worked incredibly hard in the last few months and we are very keen to get out there and show our faithful fans what we are capable of,' said Fleck after the announcement of the squad in the days leading up the tournament.

Perhaps things had been going too well in the Stormers' preparations. In a warm-up game against the Lions ten days before the season was scheduled to start, they lost two important players to injury. The promising winger Leolin Zas broke his leg and had to be stretchered off the field, while Juan de Jongh tore his medial collateral ligament and would miss the next ten to twelve weeks.

The administrators were able to hire some players to fill the vacancies at short notice, but that didn't solve the captaincy problem, which had been a bit confusing in the previous season. Juan de Jongh and Frans Malherbe had been co-captains, while Schalk Burger had also been a steadying presence in the squad during 2016. But he wasn't part of the setup any more, having signed a two-year contract with Saracens, and management felt that it was time for two of the senior players from the new crop to step forward. They announced that Siya Kolisi would be captain and Eben Etzebeth would be vice-captain. 'Although still quite young, Siya is already an experienced player who has matured both on and off the field and is one of the most popular and respected players in our squad,' said the coach.

Siya was humbled by the honour. To lead a team was not something that he was used to doing. 'There have been some great players who have led the Stormers out at Newlands, so for me to be among them is a great privilege and also a great responsibility,' he said, in a shy, formal statement. 'With the support of Eben and the rest of the senior players in the squad, I am confident that we can create something special that the fans can be proud of.'

Despite the fact that Siya had been so successful in so many teams over the years, he hadn't been thought of as 'captain material' at school or in the junior Springbok squads. But his popularity among the players, his easy-going attitude and his newfound maturity suddenly made him feel like the natural choice for the position.

The season kicked off with a decisive Stormers win over the Bulls by 37 to 24, then a similar scoreline against the Jaguares, and a 10–41 thrashing of the Southern Kings in Port Elizabeth. In fact, the Stormers kept winning until Round Eight of the competition when they went down to the Lions by 29 points to 16.

The Lions were on fire in 2017 and they were scorching any team that crossed their path. Elton Jantjies finished the season as the top points scorer in the competition, with 197 points, and the Lions lost only once all season: 36–24 to the Jaguares in Round Three. They ended the season on top overall with 65 points, closely followed by the Crusaders on 63, and then the Stormers in third position with 43 points. None of the other teams even managed to get over 40 points.

Once again, the Stormers had earned themselves a home quarter-final, this time against the Chiefs. In the previous two seasons they had been eliminated at this stage of the competition. They were determined to go further this time.

In front of their home fans, the Stormers battled hard. The game was so evenly matched that there were no points scored in the first 22 minutes, until SP Marais scored the first penalty of the game for the Stormers. But the Chiefs equalised on the half-hour mark and then pulled away with two more penalties to go into half-time leading 9–3.

After the break, the Stormers came out energised and looking to get the basics right. They ran the ball through a number of phases, driving the Chiefs all the way back to their own line. Deep in the right-hand corner of the field, Dewaldt Duvenage picked up from the breakdown, feinted one way, then released the ball to the blindside where EW Viljoen drew in an attacker and then released. Siya came steaming in from out of nowhere, caught the ball, and fell over the line right in the corner. It was a try for the Stormers from the captain, but SP Marais couldn't convert. They were back to within one point of the Chiefs.

But when the Stormers backline strayed offside a few minutes later, the Chiefs earned a penalty and opened the gap again with another three points. Time was running out and the Stormers were desperate to score. They camped out deep in the Chiefs half for the next ten minutes of the game but just could not get over the line and had to settle for a penalty.

With five minutes remaining, only one point separated the two teams. Whoever scored next would be into the semis. The Stormers were caught napping in their own 22 when flyhalf Aaron Cruden released a perfectly weighted long pass high over the heads of his backline to the wing, who was unmarked and scrambled easily over the line.

And that's how it ended: 11–17 to the Chiefs and yet another home defeat in the knockout phase of the competition for the Stormers. But the Lions were flying the South African flag high. After squeezing past the Sharks in the quarter-finals, they put on a magnificent display against the Hurricanes in the semi-finals, beating them 44–29, and in the final came close to upsetting the favourites, the Crusaders. Only a try from All Blacks captain Kieran Read separated the two teams at the end of the day.

* * *

Reflecting on his first season as captain, Siya was not unhappy with the results. His team had won 10 of the 15 games they had played and they had developed into a tight-knit group of players with great team spirit. He could say with some certainty that he had earned the respect of both the players and the fans. But there wasn't a lot of time for contemplation or looking backwards. Barely a month after the Super Rugby tournament ended, the Springbok squad was called back to duty to prepare for the upcoming Rugby Championship against New Zealand, Australia and Argentina.

Nobody had forgotten the disasters of 2016, but everyone was desperate to turn a new page and rebuild the pride and morale of the Springbok brand. Allister Coetzee knew that his job was under threat if the team didn't perform that year, as did every other member of the management team. There was a welcome sense of determination and purpose as the season kicked off. Siya had not been part of the team that had performed so badly in 2016, but he felt the pressure as much as anyone else in the squad.

In the first match of the tournament, the All Blacks announced their intentions straight away with a commanding defeat of Australia in Sydney, scoring over 50 points in a game against the Wallabies for the first time ever.

On 19 August, the Boks went up against Argentina in Port Elizabeth for their opening game. They had lost to the Pumas for the first time a year previously and needed to reassert their dominance so that everyone could see that the loss was a one-off and not 'the new normal'.

Two penalties off the boot of Elton Jantjies settled the nerves, then a debut Test try from Courtnall Skosan through some individual magic helped the Boks to go into half-time with a healthy 23–8 lead.

A couple more quality tries from both teams after the break meant the game was still evenly balanced, although the Boks were managing to retain a small lead. In the 65th minute the Boks were leading 23–15 and on the attack when they took the ball far out left, dragging the Pumas with them, and then quickly moved it to the right, where Siya was in the line with plenty of space. With the ball in hand, he ran from the 22-metre line across the try line, then cut back and dived to score under the posts.

One more try at the death made the final score 37–15, and the Boks could say justifiably that they were back on track. Things had been looking up since June, when Allister Coetzee's men had dismantled the touring French side with three solid wins in a row. They had scored 35 points or more in each of those three games. Siya had scored a beautiful try in the second Test, played in Durban on 17 June, and had been named man of the match.

Many critics suggested this was Siya's best game in a Springbok jersey. He was ferocious in defence and at the breakdowns and his try was incredible. He intercepted the ball, managed to just keep it off the grass, and ran 22 metres to score in a brilliant solo effort.

In his early years, Siya had made his name as a brick wall on defence. That never changed, but as the years flew by, he got better and better on the burst, his ball-handling improved, and he showed himself to be surprisingly effective when joining the backline.

The win against Argentina in the Championship made it four victories in a row for the Springboks, and there was a growing sense that they had turned their fortunes around.

A week later the two teams faced off again, this time in the city of Salta in Argentina. The Springboks wore an unfamiliar bright orange uniform for the game but played with the same green-and-gold flair that the fans were used to. Siya had a particularly good game, scoring twice with some free-wheeling, expansive play. The Boks were playing a very open game, and Siya joined the line again and again to find space, gather the offload, and keep the momentum going. Although Argentina came back with a pair of well-executed tries, the Springboks were never going to lose this one and they sauntered home by 41 points to 23, with Siya being named man of the match.

It was great to get two wins from two games but everyone knew that the big challenges still lay ahead, in the form of Australia and New Zealand. From Argentina, the team travelled on to Perth, in Australia, to prepare for the first match against the Wallabies. The team was settled and growing in confidence. They boasted massive power in the form of Tendai

Mtawarira, Malcolm Marx and Coenie Oosthuizen in the front row; Eben Etzebeth and Pieter-Steph du Toit as locks; Siya and Jaco Kriel taking up flanking positions; and Uzair Cassiem rounding off the pack as eighth man.

Among the backs, coach Allister Coetzee had selected Raymond Rhule and Courtnall Skosan on the wings, Andries Coetzee at fullback, and the versatile Jesse Kriel and Jaco Serfontein as centres, with Elton Jantjies as flyhalf and Ross Cronjé at scrumhalf.

With stars like Israel Folau, Kurtley Beale and Michael Hooper in the Australian team, it was always going to be a tight game, but few could have predicted quite how close it was going to be.

Elton Jantjies scored a penalty in the fourth minute. Bernard Foley replied with an Australian penalty four minutes later. Jesse Kriel scored the first try after he unloaded a smart kick downfield behind the defence that he chased and collected and went over. But the lead was lost a few moments later when inside centre Kurtley Beale showed why he was such a legend with some fancy footwork to run around the defenders and score. A second Aussie try from a fast-moving maul using massive legpower was followed by a penalty from Elton Jantjies, and a well-executed maul from a line-out on the Australian 22 that just kept on going and going, sending Springbok hooker Malcolm Marx over the line for the try.

The game was nearly won in overtime when the Springboks found Jantjies in the perfect position and he set up a drop kick, only to have it charged down by two advancing Wallabies. The game ended all square at 23–23.

After the game in Perth came the most daunting encounter in all of world rugby: a date with the All Blacks at home at the QBE

Stadium in Albany, outside Auckland. Everyone knew that the Springboks would have their backs to the wall, but this was an epic fail on a scale that no one predicted. The Springbok defence was dismantled and tossed aside by a rampant All Blacks side who seemed to be able to score whenever they felt like it.

At half-time the score was 31 to 0, and by the end the All Blacks had added another 26 points to make it 57–0, which was the largest points defeat the Springboks had ever experienced.

In truth, it could have been a lot worse. The Springboks, to their credit, never gave up, and despite a massive onslaught over the last 20 minutes, they only conceded one score during that period. But it was cold comfort after such a humiliating defeat.

Reflecting on the result, former captain Jean de Villiers remarked to SuperSport, 'It is very difficult to find something positive to say about this game. We need to be honest with our-selves, we got outplayed in every single department and were beaten by a much better team.' Once again, everyone in the rugby fraternity had a lot to say about what had gone wrong, including World-Cup-winning coach Jake White. In a col-umn for the All Out Rugby website, White said that Allister Coetzee kept making mistakes in selection and sacrificing experience for youth. 'We've discarded all of the guys who have the experience of beating the world's best teams,' opined White. 'Malcolm Marx is going to be a great Springbok, but he would get there much quicker if he was given the baton by Bismarck du Plessis.'

It was a very difficult patch for everyone involved in Springbok rugby, but even more so for the pack of forwards who formed the core of the team. Players like Marx, Etzebeth, du Toit and Mtawarira knew they were world class, and they knew they had been delivering, yet their more creative players had failed to convert all the good service into points. Once again, that responsibility fell on the coach.

There's nothing harder than coming back from such a big defeat, but the Boks responded admirably and were able to earn a hard-fought 27–27 draw with Australia two weeks later in Bloemfontein. At this point in the competition, these two teams were only playing for second place, but neither was prepared to give an inch, and the lead changed hands several times as the old rivals vied for advantage before ending again all square.

This left only one more game against the All Blacks. In their previous two meetings, the Boks had conceded 57 points in both games and they were determined not to do that again. More than that, they were playing for pride and dignity against a rampant foe.

Newlands was packed to the rafters for the final game of the Rugby Championship. The opening minutes were frenetic and the crowd was in full voice when the All Blacks' Sam Whitelock stole the ball illegally and gave up a penalty to Elton Jantjies to slot through the posts and break the duck that had been hanging over the team since the Albany game. Beauden Barrett equalised a few minutes later and the Boks were lucky to avoid another five-pointer when Rieko Ioane beat a tackle on the ten-metre line and outsprinted the whole team chasing him from the 22, but lost control at the last minute as he crashed over the line.

In the 32nd minute there was another mad scramble for the ball behind the Springbok try line, but this time the try was given and the All Blacks went up 8–3. The Springboks were losing but those fearing another wipeout began to relax a little, particularly when the Boks moved forward through 14 phases of play before Steven Kitshoff put in a mighty shove to almost score under the posts, before handing off to Ross Cronjé, who dotted down under the posts to make it eight points each.

Then some bad luck saw the team go down to another try to Ioane. With the Springboks on attack, Ross Cronjé sent a pass that deflected off a team-mate into Ioane's arms. He was already moving at speed and he just turned on the gas, leaving everyone behind, and scored again for the All Blacks. The score moved on to 15–10 in favour of the All Blacks. Siya had been less effective than he usually was on the night, and was substituted in the 54th minute, making way for Jean-Luc du Preez.

But the Boks as a unit were in this game until the end, and they were up for a fight. Handre Pollard offloaded in the tackle to Malcolm Marx, who made some ground, drew in a defender, and released Jean-Luc du Preez, who crashed gratefully over the line. With a solid conversion, the Boks were back in front 17–15 with ten minutes left to play. The Newlands crowd were absolutely losing it.

Then a brilliant piece of individual play from All Blacks fullback Damian McKenzie changed the game again. He dodged one Springbok tackle, saw a gap, and sprinted through between two other defenders and kept going all the way into the corner. The conversion was missed and the score was 22–15.

The final few minutes had all sorts of drama. Damian de Allende was sent off for a late tackle, but the Boks remained undeterred. An attacking line-out on the five-metre line, then a rolling maul that tied up the Kiwi pack, released Malcolm Marx over the line again with the ball for five more precious points. The team was so fired up that they barely celebrated, converting quickly and running back to the halfway line for the restart. But they were out of time and the game finished a very healthy 25 points to 24. 'A titanic Test Match,' said the television commentator as the final whistle blew, 'and the All Blacks win it by one.'

Another loss to the All Blacks, albeit one that was so close, stung the team. At the same time, they needed to be realistic. After all, the Springboks had beaten the All Blacks only once since August 2011, when they scraped a 27–25 win at Ellis Park in 2014. Apart from that one result, the last 11 games had all ended in a Kiwi victory. Clearly, the balance of power between the two great rugby nations had shifted in the previous decade, and if South Africa wanted to shift it again, then they were going to need to make some deep and meaningful changes to the domestic game.

It looked like the first big change that was coming was going to be in the position of head coach. Allister Coetzee's reign at the top of the game, for whatever reasons, simply hadn't produced the results that the country was looking for, and the rugby-watching public was baying for his blood. Former Springbok Rassie Erasmus, Siya's mentor in his early days with Western Province, had recently been appointed as director of rugby for SARU, and there was a sense that he would be making a move soon, but in the meantime Coetzee was still making plans for the end-of-year tour. But his win percentage was only 43 per cent across two seasons, and that simply would not do. While the pack was still strong, too many errors had crept into the team, and their basic ball-handling was not where it should have been. There seemed to be a general lack of a plan ... too much aimless kicking and chasing downfield, while the backline's ability to create moments of magic and entertainment felt like some kind of magical lost art from the golden age of rugby.

Perhaps the most obvious sign that Coetzee's reign was coming to an end was how Rassie Erasmus took a particularly hands-off approach to the Springboks. On the face of it, this could be seen as a vote of confidence in the coach – to let him do things his way. On another level, it felt like Erasmus did not want to be seen to share in the blame for what was clearly a team adrift and rudderless. Most rugby-watchers had a sense that the end-of-year tour would be Coetzee's last as Springbok coach.

But, at this exact moment, Siya had far more delightful and immediate concerns. In November, the Kolisi family welcomed a new baby girl into their lives. They named her Keziah and adjusted to living with a sixth member of the household. Rachel and Siya's Instagram feed from this time is full of delightful pictures of the little girl, walks on the beach, trips to Rhodes Memorial and family portraits, although they were careful to protect the baby's identity from the general public. But everything had gone smoothly and there was a real sense of joy that their family, with two boys and two girls, now felt complete.

In December, Siya was also honoured to be named as 2017 Players' Player of the Year at the first-ever BrightRock Players' Choice Awards in Sandton. The awards were voted on by players in all of South Africa's 14 rugby unions. It meant a lot to Siya to be recognised in this way by his fellow professionals.

* * *

There was one more tour to get through before the end of the year: a four-match series in Europe with games against

Ireland, France, Wales and Italy. If there had been any talk of a Springbok renaissance after the titanic effort they put in to nearly beat the All Blacks, that talk was extinguished with a woeful display against Ireland in Dublin on 11 November. Four tries and three conversions versus zero tries, four penalties against one – the numbers spoke for themselves. *Sport24* reported after the game: 'The Boks were abysmal. Ireland beat them in the air with well-weighted contestable kicks while South Africa's tactical kicking, from Ross Cronjé in particular, was embarrassing.' Not only did the Boks not score any tries, they didn't even look like scoring. Once again, Nick Mallett was unapologetic with his criticism, saying, 'I don't care how positive you are as a personality, there are no positives to take out of this game.'

A pair of wins against France and Italy steadied the ship somewhat, but the tour had already been defined by that blow-out against Ireland. More than 65 000 people packed into the Principality Stadium in Cardiff to witness the Boks' final game of the year, against Wales. The home fans were determined that their side would provide a good showing and the Welsh players quickly obliged. Within the first ten minutes the home team was up by 14 points after some appalling defending from the Boks, who seemed utterly clueless and constantly kicked away any possession that they had. One telling statistic from the opening quarter was that the Welsh enjoyed 78 per cent of the possession. Passes were being intercepted, kicks were not finding touch, line-out throws were failing to find jumpers ... the team just couldn't seem to gel. Finally, an easy penalty by Handre Pollard got the Springboks onto the scoreboard, but Wales replied with a second try for the debutant Hadleigh Parkes. Only then did the Springboks find their feet, and inside centre Warrick Gelant sprinted past the Welsh defence to chase and touch down the ball for his first Springbok try.

The first half ended 21–10 in favour of Wales. The second half saw a more organised, determined Springbok team come onto the pitch. Handre Pollard set up an attacking line-out in the 44th minute and then barged over the line for a try, although his conversion attempt struck the upright and bounced back into play. Ten minutes later, the Springboks earned another penalty, and once again Pollard opted to set up an attacking line-out. They executed well and this time Jesse Kriel went over for the try. Pollard converted, and the Boks were ahead for the first time in the game, by one point.

But an error from Pieter-Steph du Toit led to a penalty in the 64th minute and Wales regained the lead, and that's how it stayed all the way to the end. The Springboks had lost the final game of the year 22–24 and conceded the third straight defeat to a Welsh team in Wales.

As if to add insult to injury, on the same day, the Springbok Sevens team, playing some superb rugby, beat New Zealand convincingly 24–12 in the final of the Dubai Sevens tournament to be crowned champions. The question on many people's lips was, would rugby union ever get back to the level that the Sevens team was achieving regularly?

The Springboks returned home with their tails between their legs and many hard questions that needed answering with the next Rugby World Cup less than two years away. By early March 2018, the worst-kept secret in South African rugby became official, and Allister Coetzee was replaced as head coach by Rassie Erasmus. 'It's a huge task to coach the Springboks and I'm very privileged,' said Erasmus in the *Mail*

& *Guardian*, adding that 'I really believe that we have the players and the rugby intellectual property to turn things around and mount a serious challenge at next year's Rugby World Cup.'

Erasmus's first challenge would be a showpiece match in the USA versus Wales, followed by Tests against England and Wales at home in June. Meanwhile, Allister Coetzee took up a position in Japan with the Canon Eagles. He had been recalled from Japan prematurely to take over the Springboks, and it hadn't been much of a success, but no one doubted that, under the right conditions, and with the right club, he was a formidable coach who deserved to achieve success.

17

The First Black Captain

The 2018 Super Rugby competition kicked off with a Stormers leadership determined to make more of an impact. With Robbie Fleck retained as coach and Siya staying on as captain, the upper echelons of the team were more settled than the previous season and the planning was better as a result.

The format of the competition was changing slightly and that would have an impact on everyone. After two seasons with 18 teams, the organisers had decided to revert to the 15-team format in an attempt to streamline the length of the tournament and acknowledge that the players at this level were simply playing too much rugby. Two South African teams, the Cheetahs and the Southern Kings, and one Australian team, the Western Force, were dropped, bringing the total number of games scheduled to 127, down from 142.

It was still a massive undertaking and the Stormers named a 47-man squad for Super Rugby duty. A few of the senior players were still carrying injuries, including a shoulder for Eben, a neck for Frans Malherbe and an ankle knock for Scarra Ntubeni, but the squad worked hard during the pre-season and made plans to deal with the unavailability of some of the senior players.

The first game of the season was against the Jaguares at Newlands, and the Stormers scored a handy 28–20 victory, but after that the season never seemed to gel. Despite their best intentions, they were unable to build up any momentum and a place in the knockout rounds became harder and harder to achieve. They lost the next three games in a row, then won two, then lost another three ... it was a decidedly average season, and this was reflected in poor attendance figures at the home games and a general lack of enthusiasm about the brand of rugby the Stormers were playing. They had wanted to play a more expansive game in 2018, but that hadn't always worked out and often their movement felt a little predictable. They hadn't dominated the breakdowns like they wanted to, although the set-pieces had looked better and better as the season progressed. Nevertheless, there was a reason that no Stormers players were among the top-ten try or points scorers of the season, and the team finished a very poor 11th overall.

Once again, the Lions were the outstanding South African franchise, battling all the way into the finals before losing to the Crusaders in Christchurch.

* * *

Siya's frustration with the Stormers' performance was alleviated by some astounding news that came at the end of May: the biggest role in South African sport was his. Springbok coach Rassie Erasmus had chosen Siya as Springbok captain for the upcoming tour matches against England and Wales.

Although he was captain of the Stormers and he had known Rassie since those formative years in the Western Province Rugby Institute, it was still a shock to be included in that exclusive club of players like Francois Pienaar, John Smit and Jean de Villiers who had led the national team into battle.

The first thing Siya did was call up Rachel and tell her the news. Rachel was so shocked that she dropped the phone. 'When I told my wife, she put the phone down on me,' he said, laughing, 'but she called me back and asked me to repeat what I was saying.'

The couple were forced to keep the news to themselves for a few days until Rassie Erasmus held a press conference to announce his decision. Addressing the assembled media, he said of Siya: 'I've coached him right through the academy years, right until he played for the Stormers, so I know what he can do, I know his qualities and I know how he has grown as a man and as a captain.'

Rassie was quick to point out that the captaincy was only for the June Test matches, and that former captains such as Warren Whiteley and Eben Etzebeth were injured, 'so it's just common sense for me that he would be a good option'. It felt like the coach was trying to minimise the news so that it wouldn't overwhelm Siya, but that was like trying to hold back a flood with a mop and an old blanket. The news, and everything that it symbolised, spread around the world like lightning. South Africa had a black rugby captain.

The public response was overwhelmingly positive. Social media was flooded with congratulations from rugby fans and sports stars such as Wayde van Niekerk and Temba Bavuma. Even Mmusi Maimane, leader of the Democratic Alliance, offered his best wishes. Siya's dad was also overjoyed, though he complained that journalists were calling him all day long to ask him for comment.

Given the fraught history of transformation in South African sport since 1994, many people expected there would be accusations of tokenism, and that the coach was 'playing politics', and indeed there were some who labelled it as nothing more than a publicity stunt. But Siya shrugged it off, saying that he had known Rassie for a decade: 'I think it is a genuine appointment by coach Rassie because he is not that kind of a person.'

Siya was used to the idea that some people would label the decision as 'tokenism' or 'affirmative action' and he was experienced enough not to let it affect him. After all, Siya's entire career had taken place in an era when quotas and arguments around racial representation were the backdrop to every South African team. Athletes of colour who made it to the top of their game in South Africa, no matter what their sport, invariably had to endure questioning by small-minded people over whether they *really* deserved to be there. It was infuriating and depressing, but those were the cards that this era of professional sport had dealt them. Most players found ways to ignore the naysayers and just do what they did best. During a press conference following the announcement of his captaincy, Siya noted that all he wanted to do 'to reward coach Rassie is to make sure that I deliver on the pitch'.

It wasn't only on the pitch that Siya was making an impact. He entered into an exciting partnership with the Japanese technology giant Panasonic. His commercial agent, Kendra Houghton, had seen a flood of companies approaching Siya for endorsements and brand association, but she was wary of getting him too involved with anything off the field. 'I could sell him every single day but he has very little time off,' she said, and his time was important for relaxation and family.

Nevertheless, Panasonic made a compelling pitch to Siya, and their plan really appealed to him. Working with the Nelson Mandela Foundation, Panasonic planned to donate over 100 000 solar-powered lights to poor South African families living without electricity. 'My agent told me about what Panasonic was doing,' he said, 'and as soon as I heard, I wanted to jump straight into it, because it's all about helping people, lifting them up and making a difference in people's lives.'

Siya remembered all too well what it was like to live in a dark, smoke-filled house, with only a candle to provide light. He was only too happy to lend his name to something that he believed could be of so much benefit to children growing up in disadvantaged circumstances.

There were other endorsements too. When a company called OpenView began offering free access to satellite television for poorer communities, Siya again jumped in and got involved. 'The idea that you can enjoy all kinds of entertainment … movies, news, sport and kids' programmes with no monthly fees is groundbreaking. Being able to access knowledge and information is important and OpenView is making that possible for millions of South Africans,' Siya said.

In another sign that his horizons were expanding, Siya got involved with the shoe company Freedom of Movement to design a veldskoen called the FOM x Kolisi. Proceeds from the shoes, made from all local materials, went towards the levelling and grassing of the rugby field at the Mbekweni Youth Centre in Paarl.

These were brand endorsements and projects that Siya passionately believed in, and that didn't take much time away from his many commitments to the Springbok cause. And that was where his priorities had to be.

* * *

In the weeks leading up to his debut as captain, Siya had a lot of time to think about the role of the Springbok captain and what it meant for the country. For a few weeks, that was all that anyone asked him. Two men who have thought and written a lot about the Springbok captaincy are Edward Griffiths and Stephen Nell. In *The Springbok Captains*, they suggest: 'For millions of white South Africans during the 20th Century, [the captain] has been a positive, strong symbol of the courage and strength they believe are so integral to their principles and their way of life; yet for millions of black South Africans, he has been a visible face of minority breast-beating and arrogance.'

Siya had the chance to shatter those stereotypes once and for all. His easy-going nature and his ability to cross cultural boundaries naturally, coupled with his prodigious talent on the field, had allowed him to skirt the issue of race for a long time. He had arrived on the scene at a time when South Africa was perhaps ready to move past race, and he embodied everything that rugby fans wanted to see in a leader. He was humble, strong, smart, religious and a wonderful all-rounder. He was welcomed into the Springbok fold with open arms. But, as captain, the questions of race and quotas and the politics of the game were much harder to ignore. 'To be Springbok captain is to live under pressure,' write Griffiths and Nell, and to be the first black Springbok captain would increase that pressure exponentially.

But Siya was ready for it. His solid family foundation, his close relationship with his team-mates and his long history with Rassie were sources of great comfort and reassurance as he headed into the first few games as captain. The Springbok leadership had accepted the fact that there needed to be a racial quota in the team, but they were confident that the talent pool was big enough to let them deal with the issue seamlessly. As Liz McGregor writes in *Springbok Factory*, 'judging the levels of racial progress in rugby by the colour of the national team is superficial and counter-productive. It puts unfair pressure on the national coach and the players themselves, and it saps emotional energy from a team because they are forced to think of themselves in racial terms, and to compete with each other on the basis of race, when everything in the dynamics of a successful team works in the opposite direction ... of seamless brotherhood.'

Siya had the privilege of experiencing what a great Springbok captain could do for a player on his team. When he made his Springbok debut in June 2013, Jean de Villiers was still captain. McGregor writes: 'In the week leading up to the game, De Villiers shared a room with Kolisi. Any Bok with more than 50 caps is entitled to his own room, a cherished privilege which De Villiers voluntarily gave up in order to give Kolisi as much support as possible in the fraught build-up to the biggest game of his life.' This was the game in which Siya excelled and earned the man-of-the-match award, and a lot of credit for that performance should go to De Villiers. That was the kind of captain that Siya wanted to be.

He had no desire to give flowery speeches that would move the players. What he was going to do was lead by example in every minute of every game, first into battle and showing his troops the way. That would be the legacy of Captain Kolisi.

Steph Nel believes Siya is a great and transformative choice as captain: 'He's not a talker, he leads from the front. He's the braveheart warrior and that's how he inspires people.'

* * *

The first order of business for the new-look Bok side under Rassie Erasmus was an exhibition match against Wales, scheduled to be played in Washington, DC. It was a strange affair, and because it fell outside the official Test window, neither country was able to send its first-string players on the tour. Seventeen of the first-choice Boks, including Siya, stayed behind to prepare for England's three-match tour of South Africa.

There was plenty of outrage among commentators that the Wales game was even taking place. 'I don't know why it was organised at all,' said former Welsh captain Gwyn Jones, 'I think the game against South Africa in Washington is an absolute shambles.'

Nevertheless, the fixture went ahead, and there were immediately headaches for the new Bok coach as the team went down 22 points to 20 without displaying the kind of fight and composure that Erasmus wanted to bring back to the team. But no one read too much into the result, and instead focused on the first England game, at Ellis Park on 9 June.

This was when Rassie Erasmus's true side would be revealed and the public would get their first opportunity to see their new captain playing in an international fixture on home soil. Siya led the team with tremendous courage and skill in an epic fightback that they won 42–39 after England had scored three tries in the first 15 minutes of the game and taken a lead of over 20 points.

A week later, the two teams met again in Bloemfontein to take up the battle. Once again, England took an early lead with two tries in the first ten minutes, but they were unable to close out the game and let the Boks creep back into it. In fact, the Springbok team came back strongly and prevented England getting any more points on the board after the 12th minute of the game. In the 23rd minute, Beast made a line break, and when he was finally brought to ground, the charge was taken up by Duane Vermeulen, who was able to beat three defenders and score a classic Springbok try. Handre Pollard converted the try and then added another nine points through three penalties, before a penalty try was awarded ten minutes after the break to make it 23–12.

That's the way the scoreline stayed all the way to the end. The Boks put up a heroic defence, and Siya was able to walk off the field with two victories from two games as captain. For England, it was an entirely different story – a fifth straight Test defeat for Eddie Jones's team.

On 23 June, Jones and his men were back at the ground where he had left the Stormers in the lurch a few seasons earlier. The Newlands fans would have liked nothing more than to see their players hand Eddie Jones a kick in the pants, but that wasn't to be the case.

The third game of the England tour was a very differ- ent affair from the first two. The wet and stormy conditions meant that the game resembled trench warfare more than the free-flowing rugby of the previous encounters. The ball was slippery, the ground was muddy, and both teams dug in hard to control territory before sending high balls like mortars into enemy territory. The Boks scored a penalty in the 40th minute, followed by a hard-won try to Jesse Kriel in the 45th minute. But they weren't playing well and were penalised again and again. England captain Owen Farrell made them pay for it and slowly began to build a big score. Six successful penalties from six attempts saw the game creep out of reach for the Springboks before a late try from man of the match Jonny May sealed their fate. The final score was 10–25 and England had a rare away win in South Africa. 'Today we got a couple of disappointments and we handled them much better,' said Jones. 'That's what's called experience.'

While they may have won the series, that didn't stop South Africa from slipping from fifth to sixth place in the World Rugby Rankings, while England, despite losing the series, managed to gain two places to go into fourth position. But there was a great sense of satisfaction in the Bok camp that the first series under new leadership had gone well and the rot had been stopped. The Springboks said goodbye to each other and headed back to resume Super Rugby duties for their respective home teams.

* * *

Siya and Rachel had been well known before, but the Springbok captaincy catapulted things to a new level. It was international news that South Africa had a black captain, and every news outlet in the world relished the chance to tell Siya's story. Magazines and TV shows were constantly pitching photoshoots and magazine spreads, and the couple's social media following was growing every day. It was a wild ride for both of them but they seemed to be enjoying the attention.

Online, more and more people were projecting their ideas of what Siya and Rachel's marriage was really about, commenting on how they would behave in an interracial relationship, and somehow trying to pretend that they really understood the dynamics at play in this unique, successful, very South African family. That's not to say that it was all marital bliss all the time. Every couple have their flashpoints, gripes, worries and stresses, especially when their relationship involves long periods of time away from one another in different cities and countries. There's no way that the Kolisis were immune to that kind of pressure.

Rachel was also building her fitness brand and becoming the kind of athlete that she had always wanted to be. People tend to forget that Rachel was the one who really encouraged Siya to take his training, diet and lifestyle to the next level, and she demanded the same kind of commitment from hersel despite the responsibility of caring for four children. She was focused on cycling, running and gym, and tried to use her prominent social media profile to bring awareness to things she cared about. In March 2018, she took part in the Extreme Ride for Hunger, an epic team-cycle challenge in which riders cycle over 1000 kilometres between Kimberley and Cape Town to raise funds for feeding charity Meals on Wheels.

The ride was hard and long, and sometimes it probably felt like it would never end, but it was so much more than that. Through the rain and the sun, the wind and the dark, the team of riders and their backup crew soldiered on, seeing a side of South Africa that few people ever get a chance to see. They met amazing people along the way and saw how Meals on Wheels made such a difference in their lives. Rachel knew all about Siya and his life as part of a team, and this was her chance to have that experience too. At the end of the race, Rachel was overcome with emotion and gratitude for what had been achieved, and Siya shared a moment in which Rachel seems to be in prayer and giving thanks: 'So proud of you Mama @ rachel_kolisi! Now you and the team @extremeride4hunger can rest knowing there's a lot of people with meals for a while!' Rachel didn't stop there.

She was also training for the Two Oceans Marathon and using her social media presence to promote healthy attitudes about the body. In late June 2018, however, Rachel saw something on TV about Siya that set her off, and she responded aggressively on social media. The trigger was a comment that no one would have remembered if she had let it slide. But it caught her at the wrong time and she said something back, and the scandal-hungry masses on social media took it and ran with it. In the blink of an eye, there was a Twitter storm of opinion and comments and thinkpieces about whether other women had the right to comment on married men, and about cultural norms and expectations around men and women. Like most social media controversies, the whole thing was blown completely out of proportion. But Rachel took it hard: she cancelled her Twitter account and dramatically cut back her social media presence.

18

▬

A Championship for the Ages

The seventh edition of the Rugby Championship kicked off on 18 August, with the four regular teams back in competition for southern hemisphere dominance. What was different about this year's competition? It would be the final full championship before the 2019 Rugby World Cup in Japan, which meant it was the last chance for teams to establish dominance against their southern hemisphere peers, and to see how they measured up. The 2019 version of the competition would be abbreviated and it was assumed that the teams would play conservative rugby to ensure that no further injuries were picked up before the World Cup. So, the 2018 Championship was going to be an all-or-nothing affair.

Argentina, South Africa and Australia were all looking for an opportunity to measure themselves against the mighty All Blacks. After all, the New Zealanders were five-time winners of this competition, as well as being winners of the last two World Cups. They were indisputably the best rugby team in the world. Great rivalries have come and gone over the years, and will no doubt rise again in some distant rugby future, but at this point in the evolution of the game, the All Blacks were setting new standards of success in professional sports.

Behind the scenes, SA Rugby had been working hard on building systems, supporting their players, and trying to implement long-term thinking when it came to managing their most important assets – the players.

They came up with a good plan, but it came with a cost, and that cost would be that short-term results would not always be positive when the goal was long-term success. Rassie Erasmus understood that the team had fewer than 15 games in total to play before the World Cup kicked off, and he needed to gain a far deeper understanding of his squad to see who he could rely on when push came to shove in a high-intensity World Cup situation.

He needed to see new players play under real pressure, to try out different combinations, and to let the younger players experience rugby at the highest level before the World Cup began. So, even though the Rugby Championship matches felt like life and death on the weekends when they were being played, in reality they were used in service of a greater goal – the World Cup. The Springboks could have played their best team every week of the tournament – many fans were baying at them to do so – but they had a plan and they stuck to it.

In a long television interview on SuperSport with veteran rugby journalist Matthew Pearce after the series, Erasmus shared his vision of how he was approaching the job of coaching the team. 'There's a choice between crisis management style where you try to win the next match on your plate at whatever cost, or you can take a more long-term view,' he said. He was taking the long view, trusting that the fans would see how they were building up the squad: 'People are prepared to take a wait-and-see approach.'

* * *

On the first game day in August, Siya was captaining the Springboks as they took on Argentina, while New Zealand hosted Australia. At Kings Park in Durban, Damian Willemse and Marco van Staden made their debuts for the Boks. This was the stadium where the Pumas had beaten the Boks for the first time ever back in 2015, and the men from Argentina were keen to repeat that epic upset in 2018.

The Springboks scored first through Lukhanyo Am's try in the eighth minute. He latched on to some great handling and passing between Andre Esterhuizen, Frans Malherbe and Faf de Klerk and powered across the line. Argentina equalised after a few minutes when Willie le Roux spilled a high ball that Nicolás Sánchez was able to grab and run in under the posts, then convert it for two extra points.

A few minutes later, Siya found himself in possession with some space down the wing and he made a fantastic break before being reeled in. But he was isolated, and when he released the ball the Pumas effected a counter-ruck and made the turnover, then the winger Ramiro Moyano ran 20 metres and passed beautifully to his team-mate Pablo Matera, who charged across the final ten metres and touched down for the try. It was 14–5 to Argentina.

In the 31st minute, Willie le Roux more than made up for his earlier blunder. He caught the ball on the 22, looked up and across the field and delivered a delightful little kick over the defence. It hung in the sky just long enough for Aphiwe Dyantyi to race in between two defenders and wait for it with open arms, then twist and run across the line, without anyone laying a finger on him, for his second try in the green and gold.

195

Four tries in the first 40 minutes of an action-packed Test match. With the half-time score at 14–10, both teams had everything left to play for.

After the break, it was Aphiwe Dyantyi again who made all the difference. Scrumhalf Faf de Klerk sent a high ball behind the Puma defence and down the left wing. The bounce of the ball sat up nicely for a chasing Dyantyi, who had the pace to get past the defender, who tackled him desperately. Dyantyi went to ground a few yards short of the line but managed to maintain control and scoot forward over the whitewash for a second try.

Six minutes later, Malcolm Marx nearly got over, then Beast Mtawarira got even closer before being brought down on the line. The ball was recycled to Siya, who also went close, and then it came out a fourth time when Faf de Klerk sent a long pass all the way out to the wing, where Makazole Mapimpi crossed the try line with ease.

This was followed by a brilliant backline move from the Boks that hopelessly exposed the Argentinian defence. Dyantyi could have gone over himself for a hat-trick right there, but he kept the ball moving down the line all the way to the end to Mapimpi, who got his second try.

Argentina came back with one more try in the 66th minute and the game was in the balance once again, but a smart try from Faf de Klerk in the 69th minute sealed a 34–21 victory for the Boks.

In Round Two, New Zealand cruised past Australia again with a winning margin of 28 points. Beauden Barrett scored four tries himself and the team racked up seven in total to Australia's one. The Springboks watched the game on TV with a sense of foreboding, but they had more immediate concerns to deal with, namely, the return match against Argentina in the city of Mendoza. Rassie continued to experiment with the lineup, picking Franco Mostert over Pieter-Steph du Toit, who started on the bench.

The Springboks started well but Argentina edged ahead with an early penalty after Frans Malherbe was penalised for not releasing the ball. In the 13th minute, Siya joined the line at outside centre and watched as the Springboks swung the ball down the line moving from left to right. He collected the ball just beyond the 22-metre line, bounced off a defender, and found himself with some space. Siya ran hard, fast and straight. He looked around for support but he was all on his own with two defenders to beat, so he sold a beautiful little dummy to the left and then darted right before crashing gratefully over the line. It was a great solo effort from the captain to take his team ahead and score his fourth international Test rugby try.

Argentina came back with a great try when they opened up the Springbok defence and got into a two-on-one situation that allowed enough space for Bautista Delguy to score in the corner. After that, the Springboks were unable to hit back and they paid the price with some poor tackling that saw the Argentine backline progress from the halfway line and over the whitewash for a second try from Delguy. The momentum in the game had shifted, and two more tries from Argentina appeared to put the nail in the coffin of the Springboks. At half-time they were down by 20 points, but a first Test try for Lionel Mapoe, after some brilliant interplay between Warren Whiteley, Aphiwe Dyantyi and Willie le Roux, gave the team hope and they attacked valiantly for the last 15 minutes. But it was no use. The Argentinian defence held fast and the game ended 32–19 to Argentina.

It stung to lose again to Argentina, this time by quite a wide margin, but there was also a grudging respect for the South Americans, who had been improving steadily for many years and who were now genuinely a first-class team.

The sense of apprehension around meeting the All Blacks only increased when they dismantled Argentina 46–24 in the first match of Round Three to win their third game in a row of the competition. They nearly managed 50 points and never looked in trouble.

For the Boks' first game against Australia the experimentation continued. The coach opted to give Cheslin Kolbe his Springbok debut at fullback and to bring back Pieter-Steph du Toit into the starting lineup as blindside flank, with Siya playing on the openside. Jesse Kriel, Elton Jantjies and Damian de Allende replaced Lukhanyo Am, Handre Pollard and Andre Esterhuizen in the line, while up front Steven Kitshoff started instead of Beast Mtawarira.

This was an important game for both teams. They both felt they were better than Argentina but not quite at the level of the All Blacks, so whoever won the next two clashes would feel a sense of superiority going into the 2019 World Cup. When you're in a competition with the All Blacks, the battle for second and third place becomes very important.

The match was hard-fought but it was riddled with errors from both teams, which made for unattractive rugby. By the end of the match both teams had scored two tries, Bongi Mbonambi and Makazole Mapimpi getting one apiece for the Springboks and Michael Hooper and Matthew To'omua for the Wallabies. Ultimately, it was one extra penalty and a missed conversion that was the difference between the two teams. The final score was 23–18 to Australia. The Springboks were bitterly disappointed. Their campaign had started off well, but back-to-back losses did not bode well for their first match against New Zealand.

*　*　*

The big clash in Wellington on 15 September was going to be a telling indication of how much progress the Springboks had made under Rassie Erasmus. Preparations for this game were more intense than ever. For any team, it's important to have structures that keep the rest of the world out and let the players really drill down into the specifics of the game plan. Former captain Gary Teichmann describes it well, talking about 'the team management's ability to construct a cocoon around the coaches and players, efficiently insulating the team from the infighting, instability and tantrums typical of South African rugby admin over the years. This [cocoon] meant that the Springbok coach and players were able to ignore such shenanigans, stay focused, and concentrate entirely on the business of winning games.'

Jake White had been very good at creating the cocoon, and so was Rassie Erasmus. The Springboks knew what they had to do and they knew how to do it. All they needed was a great day in the field and a little luck and they could slay the Kiwi dragon, which had been lording it over the Boks for nearly a decade.

The Springboks felt that there was enough depth in their squad that they could ask the starting lineup to give everything for an hour, then rotate them out of the game for the last 20 minutes. Siya, Eben Etzebeth, Frans Malherbe, Malcolm Marx and Steven Kitshoff – all expected to leave the field before the end of the game. It was good, simple man management.

What Rassie Erasmus was really bringing to the team was a sense of transparency and goodwill that quickly emanated throughout the structures. There were no factions, no hidden agendas ... it was all about radical honesty. The team sheet for the game the following Saturday was put up on Monday morning for everyone to see. Team selection was discussed in front of everyone so the players all knew where they stood. The coach told an interviewer that 'when players are in synch with you, they don't stress about it'. Nevertheless, a string of losses is viewed as unacceptable for any national team, and even Rassie Erasmus was not immune to pressures. Around this point in the season, he admitted that he was worried about keeping his job, and it became increasingly difficult to stick to his plan.

Planet Rugby previewed the game in the days leading up to it, and concluded: 'The All Blacks will be brimming with confidence when they take on the Springboks in their Rugby Championship clash in Wellington on Saturday.' *SA Rugby* magazine was even more brutal in its assessment of the game, telling its readers to 'banish any thoughts of some miracle victory', and ending off by saying the best the Boks can hope for is to 'avoid a hammering'.

To be fair to the writer of that piece, the statistics going into the game made for some horrific reading. The Springboks had lost the last eight consecutive games. They hadn't managed more than 20 points in any of those games. New Zealand had a win rate of 87 per cent at the Westpac Stadium. If you were a betting man, all the smart money would be against the Springboks.

But the All Blacks management were savvy enough to recognise that the Boks were gearing up for an epic clash. Assistant coach Ian Foster said: 'They love the collision, they're tough there, they carry hard. They take a lot of pride in their set-piece work and they've got some backs that really enjoy space out wide if we give it to them. They've got a lot of speed.'

Everything was set up for a real classic on a perfect night in Wellington as the Springboks stood up tall in their green tracksuits and honoured the haka moments before the match got under way.

* * *

Game on. In the first few minutes of play, every Bok fan's worst nightmare seems to be coming to life. The Kiwi handling of the ball is just so superb that their attacks keep on coming. Aaron Smith's pass down the line is deflected, but Beauden Barrett crouches low, takes the ball and instantly flicks it to his brother Jordie, who is bursting through the line next to him; it looks almost like they're telepathic. Jordie is unopposed and runs over the first try of the match, but his older brother misses the conversion: 5–0 to New Zealand. A few minutes later and the All Blacks' incredible ball-handling skills are on display again. A gap opens down the right for winger Ben Smith, who explodes past the defence then passes inside to Aaron Smith for another All Blacks try, which is converted, taking the score to 12–0. Unless the Springboks make a move soon, the game will fast become unwinnable. Salvation arrives in the form of a try after the ball is moved from Faf de Klerk to Malcolm Marx to Willie le Roux to Aphiwe Dyantyi, who races over the line, cuts back in, and keeps going all the way under the posts.

Handre Pollard converts and the Boks are back in the

game. They pile on the pressure for the next 15 minutes, and it pays off with the unthinkable: the All Blacks make a rare mistake. It all starts with Aphiwe Dyantyi collecting a little dab through from Willie le Roux. As he is caught by Beauden Barrett, he kicks forward but the ball rolls into touch. Spontaneously, Jordie Barrett takes a quick line-out and throws a long shaky ball into the middle of the pitch to no one in particular. The bounce favours Willie le Roux, who manages to grab onto the ball before Rieko Ioane gets there, and darts across the line for a try, much to the enjoyment of the rapturous crowd.

The TV cameras cut to a shot of the Springbok management team; all four members are pumping their fists and screaming, 'Yes', yes, yes!' There is a real sense now that the Springboks are in it, that they have come looking for a fight, and that they have banished the fear of their exalted opposition.

Now we're at the half-hour mark and the All Blacks are defending on their five-metre line. A huge maul is in place and at first there is no movement, but then the Boks start to make progress – at first centimetres, then metres, and Franco Mostert is being squeezed out of the top of the maul like toothpaste out of a tube. Malcolm Marx is at the back of the maul, holding on to the ball and waiting for his moment. Then it comes: the maul collapses and he darts around the blindside with defenders desperately clawing at him and dots down. 'He has the try! Brilliant South Africa!' screams the commentator.

Then Ioane does some more damage for the All Blacks. Every time he has an inch of space, he really makes it count, and there's no catching him as he goes over for the All Blacks' third try. It's still only the first half and there is everything to play for. Handre Pollard adds three more points from a penalty and the Boks go into the break leading 24–17.

What the Boks really need is a score after the break to prevent the All Blacks from reeling them back in, and that's exactly what they get. Just 90 seconds after the break and the All Blacks have a penalty advantage. They start swinging the ball down the line towards the left wing. Cheslin Kolbe is waiting and watching as the ball gets closer and closer and into the hands of outside centre Anton Lienert-Brown. He delivers a pass to the winger and Kolbe makes his move, reaching up high to grab the ball and then belting it downfield to score. There's no one in the world who could have caught Kolbe at that particular moment. He dots down so fast that he falls into a forward somersault and lands on his feet for his first-ever Springbok try. What a moment for the young star! He read the moment brilliantly in just his second-ever Test match and lets the coach know in no uncertain terms that he is here and ready for the big moments.

Siya's men are now two scores ahead of the All Blacks with 30 minutes to play. But, once more, Ioane is causing havoc. A loose ball is bobbling on the wing; he picks it up and conjures up a moment out of nothing, squeezing through for his second try and the All Blacks' fourth on the night. Beauden Barrett converts and it's 31–24.

The Springboks need a big response and they get it in the form of a fantastic group effort. In the centre of the field, Faf de Klerk starts the next move, passing to RG Snyman, who comes round the corner and offloads in the tackle to Steven Kitshoff, then to Elton Jantjies, who sees some space on the wing. He skips a player and lofts a high ball to Warren Whiteley, who gathers in midair and passes to Aphiwe

Dyantyi as he hits the ground. Dyantyi is running out of space on the wing, but his first step is so deft and so quick that it changes everything. He lands on his left foot and executes a devastating sidestep that leaves Beauden Barrett clutching at ghosts, and then he's over for his second try. 'What a way to hit back,' screams the commentator. Dyantyi is bellowing like a professional wrestler and there is a full-blown riot in the Springbok management box. This is what it feels like when David slays Goliath.

The only bad news is that there are still 20 minutes to go and anything can happen. It is unclear whether a 12-point cushion is enough to fend off the Kiwis. A big line-out on the Springbok five-metre line develops into a solid maul. Sam Whitelock has the ball and holds it up while his team-mates grind forward. The Springboks are fractured and can't come together to mount a defence, and then the All Blacks have their fifth try, courtesy of Codie Taylor. But Barrett misses the conversion and the Springboks still have a seven-point cushion as the clock ticks down.

As if the game doesn't have enough drama, suddenly Willie le Roux is sin-binned for going offside and a late tackle on the scrumhalf following Warren Whiteley's heroic chasedown and tackle to stop a near-certain try.

Fourteen men on the field. Fifteen minutes to go. The Boks have their backs to the wall, defending furiously like they're the last Free Men protecting the castle at Winterfell from rampaging White Walkers. Finally, there is a breach in their exhausted defences and the pack simply rumble over the Springboks and collapse with the ball over the line. The try is awarded to Ardie Savea, and now only two points separate the teams. The New Zealand supporters sense that their team is going to do it again, just like they've gotten used to over years and years of last-minute victories.

Beauden Barrett has a chance to level the score but his kick skews to the right and crashes against the upright. The rugby gods are smiling down on the Springboks.

The battle rages on into the last minute. The buzzer goes but the ball stays alive, and for two and a half agonising minutes the Springboks must defend while the All Blacks storm their line. One more charge at the line, five metres out, and the ball goes to Damian McKenzie, who is charged by Aphiwe Dyantyi. McKenzie drops the ball, and the crowd screams in agony. Willie le Roux is back on the field. He picks up the ball and hoofs it into the stands. Victory! Sweet, precious victory against the best in the world.

Eben Etzebeth is screaming like a man possessed; Faf de Klerk has Handre Pollard pinned down to the ground. Everyone is going mad. It's the first time the Boks have ever won at the Westpac Stadium, the first time they've won in Wellington since 1998, and grown men are openly weeping tears of joy and relief.

Who knows how Siya is feeling after years of giving his all on the field but being denied the biggest victories when it really mattered? This feels like a life-changing moment in his career and in the trajectory of the Springboks. No one gave them a hope before this game, but they didn't let that stop them. It feels like they've won the World Cup.

* * *

When the dust had settled, the team looked back at the astonishing stats of the game. The Boks had enjoyed only 25 per cent of the possession. They had spent most of the game trapped in their own half. But they had made a jaw-dropping 235 tackles in the match, compared to only 61 by the All Blacks. It was a masterclass in defence that harked all the way back to the Western Province Rugby Institute, when the boys learned that defending is what makes the difference between great teams. They were amazing on attack, no doubt, and to score 36 points with only 25 per cent of possession is fantastic, but the story of the night was the story of teamwork and passionate defence.

Gary Teichmann is one of the few people who has experienced this kind of a game and has the storytelling ability to get it across. He writes, 'it is hard to convey the brutality of the big hits around the fringes of the scrum and the midfield. it is hard to convey the degree of planning before an international, the level of concentration required to be in the right place at the right time, the kind of courage required to place your body in the path of a muscular, charging opponent.'

It may have felt like a cup final but the fact of the matter was that the team needed to be back at work a few days later, and looking ahead to the next game against Australia. They were cheered by the fact that the Aussies had gone down against Argentina on the same day South Africa beat the All Blacks, so they had the psychological advantage going into the game at Nelson Mandela Bay Stadium in Port Elizabeth on 29 September.

Against Australia, the Boks started off beautifully. On attack in the first minute, the wily Australian Kurtley Beale tried to throw a long pass out to the wing, which Aphiwe Dyantyi anticipated, intercepted, and put down for a try with under a minute on the clock. Handre Pollard converted and the Boks were up 7–0. Siya defended courageously through the game and also did brilliantly to win a crucial penalty in the breakdown just before half-time. Pollard also had a great day on the field, scoring 13 points in all, with two conversions and three penalties. Ultimately, his contributions proved the difference between the two teams, as Australia also scored two tries. But the final score of 23–12 gave the Boks a second victory and another confidence booster that they were moving in the right direction with a coach who understood how they should be playing.

The final round of matches was scheduled for 6 October. New Zealand versus South Africa at Loftus Versveld and Argentina versus Australia in Salta. Was it too much to expect the Springboks to beat their old rivals twice in a row? Was it realistic? Nobody could say for sure. A month earlier, you would have been laughed at for suggesting it. Now there was something in the air.

* * *

The first half was a fairly subdued affair under the lights on a clear Pretoria evening. Handre Pollard scored two penalties for the Boks, including one massive kick of over 55 metres. Those were both answered by two All Blacks penalties from Beauden Barrett, and the first half ended with six points apiece.

Just after the break, Faf de Klerk cleaned up out of a ruck, and the ball went to Steven Kitshoff, then to Pollard, then to Willie le Roux, who was playing his 50th Test for the Boks. Le Roux beat his mark and made a good 25 metres before being brought down. He was isolated but held on until Francois Louw arrived and offloaded to the line. There was another great line charge from the Boks, and this time Jesse Kriel burst through the line, put his head down, and charged for the line to score the Boks' first try of the night. The crowd went crazy when Pollard converted and the Boks were seven points up, and then Pollard added three more a few minutes later. For South Africans, it all felt like some beautiful rugby dream that you didn't want to wake up from. In the 51st minute, Siya latched onto a ball in the line and charged through, taking two defenders with him, then offloading to Damian de Allende who was in the clear and unstoppable. Try number two on the Highveld for the Springboks.

With 25 minutes to go, the Boks were 17 points up. Could this be another famous victory? Not if Codie Taylor and Aaron Smith had anything to do with it, as they combined beautifully to run half the field and score the All Blacks' first try. But the Boks didn't panic, and in the 59th minute Cheslin Kolbe somehow scraped through some desperate defending to touch down, but only after the TV officials had taken a long, hard look at the replay. The 17-point cushion was restored with only 19 minutes to go.

Once again it was Rieko Ioane who spearheaded the fight-back. Beauden Barrett threw a long pass to the wing and Ioane had enough space to turn it into five points. The Springboks held on for another ten minutes, defending desperately through 13 phases until they were exhausted, and then Scott Barrett picked up from the ruck under the posts and dived over for another score, which Richie Mo'unga converted for two more.

With five minutes to go, all the All Blacks needed was one more try. The Springboks defended desperately, but there was a sense of inevitability by this point, and in the final minute of the game Ardie Savea managed to crash over and equalise. The conversion was easy, and as the final whistle blew the scoreboard ticked over and the All Blacks had won by two points.

It was exhausting and crushing for the Springbok team, but in the days that followed they were able to get a sense of perspective. They had come within a few seconds of defeating the All Blacks twice in a row and had almost won the Rugby Championship. They had forced the whole of world rugby to reevaluate the Springboks and made sure that they would not be underestimated in the upcoming World Cup. And they had regained a sense of pride and mission under a coach and a captain who were clearly the right men at the right time for the job.

19

━━

Life in the Spotlight

Siya and Rachel's celebrity status continued to build as 2018 wound down. They were one of South Africa's glamour couples, and everyone with an event on the social calendar wanted them to be present. Siya's Instagram following had exploded to more than 150 000, while Rachel had about 50 000 followers of her own.

Many people were calling Rachel 'the first lady of SA rugby' but she just tried to carry on being herself. So, it came as a shock when, in March 2019, she posted an Instagram story that took particular aim at a woman whom Rachel claimed had been sending sexually provocative pictures to Siya's private Instagram message box. Rachel was furious and asked her followers if anyone knew how she could get hold of the person.

This was just the kind of 'scandal' that social media users live for, and it instantly blew up into another storm, with people on both sides arguing about whether what she did was right or wrong. Siya said nothing, and a few days later Rachel deactivated her Instagram account, which provoked another round of gossip and innuendo.

It wasn't just Rachel who found herself being discussed at

length by South Africans. For the first time in his career, Siya had to deal with people taking shots at him. In January 2019, as part of the work he was doing for Panasonic, Siya went to Japan where he gave an interview to the local Kyodo News channel. The interviewer asked him about Nelson Mandela, and Siya expressed how much Tata Mandela meant to him, and how he was trying to live the vision of South Africa that Madiba had worked his whole life to bring about.

Later in the interview, Siya was asked about transformation in rugby, and whether Mandela would have supported a quota system. It was a loaded question but Siya did his best to answer, explaining how much more effective such interventions are in the early stages of a player's career.

'If you're going to talk about transformation, you've gotta start in the townships,' he said. 'Imagine if I didn't go to the English school ... I wouldn't have been eating properly, I wouldn't have grown properly, and I wouldn't have had the preparation like the other boys did.' It was a measured and thoughtful answer and Siya implied that the guys who were in the Springbok team were there on their own merits and not because of any quotas. He went on to explain how tough a quota system is for non-white players: 'Are you actually there because you're good enough? Even if you are, you sometimes doubt yourself.'

The Proteas fast bowler Kagiso Rabada echoed Siya's sentiments when he told an interviewer that he believed 'at a professional level, players should be picked on merit', and that 'For me, transformation is all about getting an opportunity.' Both elite athletes were expressing the fear that people thought they were there only because of the colour of their skin and not because of their talent.

Siya had given a good answer to a difficult question, but all it really did was to provide new fodder for people who made their living stirring up outrage and controversy. All they needed was a soundbite, and they had it when Siya referred to Mandela and quotas, saying, 'I don't think he would have supported that.'

Barely hours later, South African newspapers were running sensational stories such as 'Kolisi faces online fury over racial quotas remark'. The *Cape Argus* published a number of random tweets saying things like Siya was 'already drinking from the poisoned well'.

The online storm blew up quickly, then died down. A few weeks after Rachel deactivated her Instagram account, she had a change of heart and got back online again. For both of them, no long-lasting damage had been done, but it was a good lesson in how to navigate the tides of celebrity when you're in a prominent role, especially in South Africa, where issues of race and identity still cloud every aspect of life.

Siya shrugged it off after a few days, but one person who was really upset about the whole sordid affair was Rassie Erasmus. He was fuming that his captain and friend was constantly being disrespected. Rassie told the media that to call Siya's captaincy mere tokenism was 'an insult to his intelligence'.

The coach defended Siya passionately to broadcaster Matthew Pearce, insisting that appointing him captain was 'the right thing for the team', and that the politics of it had been the furthest thing from his mind. He was just doing what was good for the side. On reflection, though, the coach admitted that he had been naive to expect it would not be such a big deal for Siya and the nation, and that perhaps he should have given Siya some time with ex-captains like Victor Matfield or John Smit to learn about Springbok captaincy before the position was thrust upon him.

There is no doubt that Siya had performed well as captain, both on the field and off, but the pressure that came with the job was relentless, and it semed that a misstep such as the Mandela furore was bound to happen sooner or later.

This show of support from his coach was important for Siya to hear. He was reassured that he had Rassie's complete and undivided support. Privately, the coach instructed Siya to keep his media and public interactions to a minimum in the run-up to the Rugby World Cup.

* * *

The Stormers' 2019 Super Rugby season kicked off with a serious reality check when they were thumped by the Bulls 40–3, but they bounced back well with three victories in a row before they had to travel overseas. Crucial points were lost in Australia and New Zealand, and it looked like the season was doomed to be a failure until the return match against the Bulls sparked a mini-revival, when the Stormers held on to a one-point lead in a closely fought game in front of their home fans.

Siya showed how he'd grown as a captain in one of the biggest games of the season, against the Crusaders. The visitors, who have dominated Super Rugby over the years, appeared to be running away with the game at one stage and were on track to record their fourth try when a refereeing error to do with a forward pass denied them, and kept the Stormers in the hunt. Trailing by 16 points to 19 with just a few minutes to go, the Stormers won a penalty that was in a kickable position but could also be used to launch an attacking lineout and a match-winning try.

It was a tough decision and it all rested on the captain. Siya thought about it and opted for the three points. Television footage clearly shows some unhappy team-mates arguing with him, and urging him to go for the try. The crowd also had the taste of victory on their tongues and made their feelings known. For a few seconds, it felt like there was going to be an on-field mutiny, but Siya kept his composure and insisted on the penalty, and Jean-Luc du Plessis calmly slotted it to register a tie just before the final whistle.

It was the kind of unpopular but practical decision that captains have to make sometimes, and Siya did well, earning praise from the opposing captain Sam Whitelock, who called it a 'smart move'.

The Stormers' campaign went off the rails the following weekend. Not only did Pieter-Steph du Toit pick up a shoulder injury that would sideline him for the next three weeks, but Siya was replaced at half-time after he injured his knee scoring a try. To lose two Springboks in one game was a mighty blow for the Stormers and no doubt added to the grey hairs sprouting on Springbok coach Rassie Erasmus's head.

The exact nature of Siya's injury was unclear, but suddenly his participation in the upcoming Springbok games was in doubt. 'I'm going to be in the brace for six weeks, which is the alternative to surgery,' Kolisi told reporter Craig Ray. 'I'm hoping to be ready to play in time for the Rugby Championship.'

Without some of their key players, the Stormers continued to battle hard and earned enough points to keep them in contention for the playoffs right until the last seconds of the regular season. Against the Sharks, they conceded a try in the dying seconds of the game to lose 9–12 and narrowly miss out on the playoffs. That game marked the end of Robbie Fleck's reign as coach of the Stormers, with veteran WP coach John Dobson scheduled to take over.

None of the South African teams made it into the semi-finals. That didn't bode well for the looming World Cup, but Rassie Erasmus took it in his stride. 'We have almost had a little bit of a pre-season, almost a month together like a Super Rugby pre-season,' he told the press, explaining that the squad was trying hard to simulate match intensity before the curtailed Rugby Championship of 2019 began.

* * *

In February 2019 Siya's perspective shifted again when he received one of the biggest acknowledgements of his life. He heard that he had been nominated for the prestigious 2019 Laureus World Sports Awards, to be presented in Monaco on 18 February.

He had been nominated in the category of 'Sporting Moment of the Year', which celebrates the moments that embody the true values of sport and its unique power to change the world for the better.

Each month of the year, Laureus acknowledges a defining sporting moment, and these are all put to a public vote at the end of the year. In July 2018, they had recognised what a phenomenal moment it had been in Siya's life, and in the life of the country, when he led the Boks onto the field at Ellis Park against England as the first-ever black Springbok captain.

Siya didn't waste much time worrying about whether he would win it or not. It was just amazing to be nominated for his role in uniting the country, and it was a welcome distraction from all the opinions that had been flying around in the wake of his Mandela comments.

It was going to be an absolutely star-studded event. Even though Siya had become used to the presence of celebrities in his life, it was still quite something to think about rubbing shoulders with Lewis Hamilton, LeBron James, Luka Modrić and many, many more global superstars in Monaco. The trip didn't exactly go to plan, though. His flight was delayed, so he missed his connection and then his luggage was lost. In desperation, Siya had to make a quick stop at a Monaco boutique to pick up a tuxedo and rush straight to the event, but he was too late to walk the red carpet.

It was a glittering event. Siya watched as awards were given to, among others, Tiger Woods (Comeback of the Year), Novak Djokovic (Sportsman of the Year), the French men's football team (Team of the Year) and Simone Biles (Sportswoman of the Year).

When it came time for his category to be announced, Siya clapped and cheered as he heard the story of Xia Boyu, a double amputee from China who had finally succeeded in climbing Mount Everest on his fifth attempt. Boyu had been climbing the mountain in 1975 when he gave his sleeping bag to another climber during a storm and suffered such severe frostbite that both of his feet had to be amputated. But he never stopped trying to climb the mountain, and in 2018 he finally succeeded. Siya was not in the least embarrassed to lose to a guy like that. It was a magical night, and he was proud of both the recognition he had received and his acceptance into the elite strata of world sports stars.

Twelve hours later, he was on a plane back to his family and his team.

* * *

Was it recognition by the Laureus World Sports Awards that unlocked a deeper understanding for many South Africans? It felt like a global acknowledgement that Siya Kolisi could become one of the greatest Springbok captains of all time. He connects effortlessly – across race, across class, across the generations. Children love him, his peers respect him, and the older generation see him as proof that change is happening and that South Africa can move forward and break the deadlock that has defined us for so long.

People see Siya as an embodiment of the nation's potential, and project onto him everything that they want to see from their country, from where it's been to where it's going. He was born into unbearably difficult circumstances and there was a strong probability, as for so many like him, that he would never find a way out. But for Siya, the one in a million, the system worked. His talent was recognised early. He was plucked out of obscurity, nurtured, and encouraged, and with God-given talent and a fierce work ethic, he shaped a new destiny and began to thrive on the global stage.

Siya may not be the kind of player who steals the spotlight, who wins all the man-of-the-match awards, and who puts lots of points on the scoreboard. But there's a reason that, in nine years of Super Rugby, he's only ever received two yellow cards and no red cards.

He is the ultimate team player, an unflappable pillar of strength with a cunning rugby brain who works selflessly for the team and for the cause. There are others who will score more points, who will generate more headlines, and who will bask in the limelight, but they thrive because Siya is out

217

there giving his whole heart and soul and putting his body on the line over and over again. There is no one out there on the field who will work harder, be braver, or commit more to the cause ... and in a team sport like modern rugby, that's all anyone can ask.

Epilogue

One late summer afternoon in January, Siya bundles his family into the car and drives across Port Elizabeth. Up Cape Road, then left into College Drive, past the familiar landmarks and back in time to the place that shaped him all those years ago.

The whitewashed buildings, the emerald-green fields and the boys in their familiar grey trousers, white shirts and blue blazers immediately transport Siya back to a time when his own future was uncertain and he was just one in a large group of nervous newpots at the beginning of their journey into adulthood.

He's driven back through the familiar gates many, many times since then, but this time is different. This time, it means even more. Siya and Rachel are bringing Liyema back to Port Elizabeth to begin Grade 8 at Grey High School. There were many great schools that Liyema could have gone to in Cape Town, but for Siya there must be something deeply symbolic and cathartic about enrolling his brother in the school that shaped his character and changed his life so profoundly.

Liyema will go on his own journey and will forge his own

path. But for Siya, to be here at the start of a new school year, back at the school with a wife and children of his own, with a stellar career in the game that he loves, enrolling his long-lost younger brother has to be a deeply emotional moment to savour.

Siya watches as Liyema says goodbye to Rachel and his siblings, then turns and receives a new tie from one of the matrics. Then he takes a final glance back at Siya and Rachel and walks through the historic entrance under the clock tower to begin his journey.

Acknowledgements

My thanks to everyone who gave of their time and told their stories about the Siya that they knew: Mr Nyoka and Lulama Magxaki of Emsengeni Primary School; Collette Molenaar, Adie Mukheibir, Holly Barnes and Gary Carter of Grey Junior and High schools; Menson Komeni, Fezi Majola, Andrew Hayidakis, Ian Rijsdijk, Nick Holton, Kendra Houghton, Jacques Hanekom, Steph Nel, Greg Hechter, JJ Fredericks, Herman Masimla, Dolla Sapeta and all the people who came forward with stories and anecdotes when they heard about the book. Special thanks to Dean Carelse for his help and generosity in sharing stories about Siya's life and career.

Last but not least, love and gratitude to my wife, Tanya, and daughters, Naomi and Sophia, for putting up with hours and hours of rugby across multiple channels and at any hour of the day and night. You went far beyond the call of duty.

Note: The events in this book about Siya Kolisi are based on fact. However, in certain scenes I have taken creative licence with dialogue and the emotional lives of the characters in the interests of creating a story that is entertaining while staying true to the known facts.

Statistics

Siya's Domestic Career (2008–June 2019)

SEASON	TEAM	COMPETITION	PLAYED	WON	DRAWN	LOST	POINTS
2008	Grey High 1st XV		17	16		1	45
2009	Grey High 1st XV		22	14		8	70
2011	Western Province	Vodacom Cup	6	4	1	1	5
2012	Western Province	Currie Cup	13	6	1	6	20
	Stormers	Super Rugby	16	14		2	5
2013	Western Province	Currie Cup	1			1	
	Stormers	Super Rugby	13	6		7	10
2014	Western Province	Currie Cup	3	2		1	
	Stormers	Super Rugby	15	7		8	5
2015	Western Province	Currie Cup	6	5		1	10
	Stormers	Super Rugby	16	9	1	6	5
2016	Stormers	Super Rugby	16	10	1	5	10
2017	Stormers	Super Rugby	13	8		5	30
2018	Stormers	Super Rugby	15	5		10	10
2019	Stormers	Super Rugby	11	5	1	5	20

Siya's International Career (2010–2018)

SEASON	TEAM	COMPETITION	PLAYED	WON	DRAWN	LOST	POINTS
2010	Baby Boks	IRB Junior World Championship	5	3	0	2	10
2011	Baby Boks	IRB Junior World Championship	3	2	1		
2013	Springboks	International Tests	2	2			
2014	Springboks	International Tests	2				
		Rugby Championship	6	4		2	
2015	Springboks	International Tests	3	2	1		
		Rugby Championship	1				
		Rugby World Cup	2	1		1	
2016	Springboks	International Tests	3	3			5
2017	Springboks	International Tests	6	3	3		
		Rugby Championship	6	2	2	2	15
2018	Springboks	International Tests	4	2		2	
		Rugby Championship	6	3		3	

Sources

Alberts, Derek. 'Growing up Grey – the Siya Kolisi story'.
Goodthingsguy.com, 7 June 2018. Available at www.
goodthingsguy.com/sport/grey-siya-kolisi-story/. Accessed on
3 July 2019.

Anonymous. 'Be their hero: Siya Kolisi and his journey to
fatherhood'. 'Guy Skills' column, *Men's Health*, 29 August 2016.
Available at www.mh.co.za/guy-skills/be-their-hero-siyas-kolisi-
journey-to-fatherhood/. Accessed on 3 July 2019.

Griffiths, Edward and Stephen Nell. *The Springbok Captains:
The Men Who Shaped South African Rugby*, third edition
(Johannesburg: Jonathan Ball Publishers, 2015).

Johannes, Lesley-Anne. '"I'm pretty strict with the kids and he's
the good guy": Rachel Kolisi talks family, sports and love'.
Parent24, 13 June 2018. Available at www.parent24.com/Family/
Family-fun/im-pretty-strict-with-the-kids-and-hes-the-good-
guy-rachel-kolisi-talks-family-sports-and-love-20180608.
Accessed on 3 July 2019.

McGregor, Liz. *Springbok Factory: What it Takes to Be a Bok*
(Johannesburg: Jonathan Ball Publishers, 2013).

Powers, Angus. 'African Bomber: the true story of Siya Kolisi'.
Downloadable PDF, 2014. Photography by Karl Schoemaker.
Available at www.sablenetwork.com/resources/siya-kolisi-true-
story.pdf. Accessed on 3 July 2019.

Ray, Craig. 'Siya Kolisi: "We represent something much bigger than we can imagine"'. Interview, *The Guardian*, 6 June 2018. Available at www.theguardian.com/sport/2018/jun/06/siya-kolisi-interview-south-africa-first-black-test-captain-england. Accessed on 3 July 2019.

SABC3 *Top Billing*. 'Siya Kolisi's beautiful wedding'. YouTube, 31 August 2016 (episode aired 25 August 2016). Available at www.youtube.com/watch?v=AElZ4AVho0w. Accessed on 3 July 2019.

Teichmann, Gary. *For the Record* (Johannesburg: Jonathan Ball Publishers, 2000).

Zeeman, Kyle. 'Twitter defends Rachel Kolisi after fan "thirsts" over Siya'. *TimesLive*, 19 September 2018. Available at www.timeslive.co.za/tshisa-live/tshisa-live/2018-09-19-twitter-defends-rachel-kolisi-after-fan-thirsts-over-siya/. Accessed on 3 July 2019.

Lightning Source UK Ltd.
Milton Keynes UK
UKHW022115191119
353861UK00009B/259/P